BI THE WAY

of related interest

Coming Out Stories
Personal Experiences of Coming Out from Across the LGBTQ+ Spectrum
Edited by Emma Goswell and Sam Walker
ISBN 978 1 78775 495 9
eISBN 978 1 78775 496 6

Life Isn't Binary
On Being Both, Beyond, and In-Between
Meg-John Barker and Alex Iantaffi
Foreword by CN Lester
ISBN 978 1 78592 479 8
eISBN 978 1 78450 864 7

In Their Shoes
Navigating Non-Binary Life
Jamie Windust
ISBN 978 1 78775 242 9
eISBN 978 1 78775 243 6

Gender Explorers
Our Stories of Growing Up Trans and Changing the World
Juno Roche
Foreword by Susie Green
Afterword by Cara English and Jay Stewart
ISBN 978 1 78775 259 7
eISBN 978 1 78775 260 3

BI
THE
WAY

—

The Bisexual Guide to Life

Lois Shearing

Jessica Kingsley Publishers
London and Philadelphia

First published in Great Britain in 2021 by Jessica Kingsley Publishers
An Hachette Company

5

Copyright © Lois Shearing 2021

A CIP catalogue record for this title is available from the
British Library and the Library of Congress

ISBN 978 1 78775 290 0
eISBN 978 1 78775 291 7

Printed and bound by CPI Group (UK) Ltd, Croydon, CR0 4YY

Jessica Kingsley Publishers' policy is to use papers that are natural,
renewable and recyclable products and made from wood grown
in sustainable forests. The logging and manufacturing processes
are expected to conform to the environmental regulations
of the country of origin.

Jessica Kingsley Publishers
Carmelite House
50 Victoria Embankment
London EC4Y 0DZ

www.jkp.com

To all bisexual activists who blazed the trail for us. In particular to those of the London bi scene, who took me under their wings and supported me when I first came crashing, wide-eyed and afraid, into this city.

To all those who come after me, may I help make the path a little easier for you to walk.

Contents

Introduction and Acknowledgements

During the 18 months in which I was writing this book, I wandered into a book shop every few days. Every time I did, I would eventually head over to the LGBTQIA+ section, or the feminism and gender section if they didn't have the former, and look for books specifically about bisexuality. I was only successful on two occasions: once in a Waterstones in Cardiff that happened to stock a copy of *Bisexuality and Queer Theory*, and once in Housmans Radical Booksellers in London, which was carrying Bi: *Notes for a Bi Revolution* and *Go the Way Your Blood Beats* (which I bought). Gay's the Word in London has also carried *Notes* in the past, but I've not been in there for a few years, so I can't attest to their current bi stock.

It was pretty disappointing. Especially because a lot of the other queer books on the shelves barely mentioned bisexuality either. It reminded me of the first time I walked into Waterstones in Brighton, not long after I'd come out to a friend for the first time, and wandered out wondering why I couldn't find that part of myself reflected on their shelves.

So, by the time of those book research trips, I was ready for the disappointment. It may have been almost ten years later, but I knew I wasn't going to find very much. Not because there aren't bi books out there (you will find many referenced in the back of this one) but because bisexuality is still considered... well, a bit too *awkward* to make public. It doesn't fit into our society's perception that everyone is straight until they realize they have feelings for the same gender when they become gay forever and always. If anyone can go from realizing that they are same-gender attracted to also having different-gender attractions, well, that could mean that anyone could be harbouring those desires, regardless of what kind of life they live and whom they date. And that's just a bit too messy.

So bisexuality is kept shushed. It's minimized, denied, and erased. Yet bi people keep existing and coming out and talking and writing about our experiences. As I mentioned, this is far from the first book about bisexuality; you just need to know where to look for all the others. The fight for bi visibility – which is the general term used for the bi+ movement's ongoing attempt to wrench open the curtains and force bi experiences, desires, and people out into the spotlight – is a war of attrition. (Some people have started using bi+ to represent that bi communities have historically been made up of multi-gender attracted people who may use different labels.) Every time a bi person comes out or speaks up about their experiences, or even speaks up for bi people (because closeted bi people are very much a part of this fight), it strikes another blow against the system that oppresses and marginalizes us. This book is one of the strikes against that system.

So what is this book? It's intended to be an introduction to bisexuality, its history, community, and movement, for people who are questioning themselves or just want more information about their identity. It is informed by resources that cover psychology, politics, sex research, culture, history, and language, all of which contribute to our understanding of our identity and orientation. It is mostly inspired by my experiences in the bi community; I have been openly bi since I was 14 (just over ten years at the time of writing), writing about bi+ issues in different modes for the last six or so years, and an activist/advocate/organizer in the bi+ community for the last four or so years. I started and now co-run a social sewing group for bi+ individuals and our allies in London called Stitch Bi Stitch. I founded the UK's first group for bi survivors of sexual and domestic violence: the Bi Survivors Network (BSN). I also run some elements of the London branch of BWithTheT, a bi/trans solidarity group. As well as this, I started the social media campaign #DoBetterBiUs and wrote the #DoBetterBiUs manifesto. I've been involved with multiple ad hoc projects in the bi community, including helping to organize the first bi+ Pride float in London Pride. Recently, I've been making videos about bisexuality with the incomparable Vaneet Mehta on our channel The AmBIssadors. So, I spend a lot of time actively participating in the bi community, and the questions in each of the chapters in this book are the questions and discussions I've had the most with newly out bi people.

This book also contains multiple interviews and stories from bi individuals in the 'Bi the way' call-out boxes. I tried to include as diverse an array of bi voices as possible for these stories, but these have been limited to people who speak English, are already aware of/active in the bi community, and have access to the internet, as this is how I connected with these individuals. I have only edited their statements for grammar/clarity purposes, leaving the rest of their words as they sent them to me. Some statements may include words or phrases about identity that may feel uncomfortable or outdated to you. I chose to leave these words unchanged as I don't consider it my place to prescribe how queer people express themselves, only to uplift those voices and viewpoints.

Despite my best efforts to make this book as universal and relatable as possible, it is inevitably limited by my privileges as much as it is informed by my experiences (after all, there's no such thing as true objectivity). So let's quickly go over those so you can understand some of my biases that will have unavoidably seeped into this text, and hopefully read this with as much awareness as possible. I was born and raised in the South of England, in a middle-class family. Although I have several illnesses, I'm not visibly disabled, so I don't experience ableist street harassment, although I do experience some ableism. This is one of my experiences that most closely mirrors being bi: not really fitting the stereotype of a marginalization enough for it to be taken seriously, while still often dealing with the trials and tribulations of not fitting the standard of being an abled, cis, straight, white man. I identify as a genderfluid woman, meaning that I'm mostly a woman (the gender I was announced at birth), but occasionally I'm not. I do always present as and am read as a woman, so I don't experience transphobia beyond having my identity erased. I am also a monolinguist, so I was only able to access resources in English. This has greatly limited this work to the experiences of bi communities in the English-speaking world, contributing to its Western bias. My most defining privilege is my whiteness, which has allowed me to move through the world with considerable ease, given how much white supremacy shapes all our lives. As our current systems of both gender and sexuality are a product of colonialism (more on that later), my whiteness and European heritage have a huge impact on my understanding of myself and my identity.

On that note, I would like to thank Maz Hedgehog for sensitivity reading this book. I'd also like to take this time to acknowledge the many people who inspire me to learn and write about bisexuality, including (but most certainly not limited to): Libby Baxter-Williams, Marcus Morgan (if I hadn't sat in on your 'how to be an activist' session at my first BiFest, none of this would ever have happened), Heron Greenesmith, Bren, Gabriel Alexa, Robyn Ochs, and Beth Sherouse. I'd also like to thank my friends, who have supported me throughout this whole process, especially: Rachel Standen, Alex Dytrych, Tom Naylor-Clements, Pip Williams, and Sophie Conner. Obviously, I owe a huge debt of gratitude to my parents and sister (it's not *the* book of words, Jess, but I hope you like it anyway). Finally, a huge thank you to Jessica Kingsley Publishers and Andrew James for giving me this opportunity.

Whilst writing this book, I had to leave a job because of my dyslexia for a second time, there was a historic global pandemic, and I got dumped. But throughout all of that, I prioritized this project. I put my heart and soul into it, because helping others to have easier access to the information and resources that took so long for me and others to find motivated me in a way I've never been before.

But here is where I, the author, bow out and hand over to you. It's now up to you, dear reader, to take whatever you can from this book and hopefully go forward more equipped and empowered to live your most authentic life. I hope it will inspire you to speak up and out for bi people, regardless of whether you decide it's the right label for you. I hope it will serve as a source of inspiration for you to do more research, write, organize, and live your best, bi-est (or not) life possible.

CHAPTER 1

Am I Bi?

U nfortunately, this book can't answer that for you.
No book, film, celebrity, friend, relative, or partner can answer that for you. Only you can know what's going on inside you, and even then, you might never be certain or able to label it.

What this book can do, however, is arm you with the knowledge of what bisexuality is and isn't, what bi experiences are like, and why people choose the label 'bisexual'. Of course, this book can't cover every bi experience or reason people call themselves bi – those are as expansive and numerous as the bi community itself – but I'm going to try to be as varied and diverse as possible to give you the best overview I can.

Lots of people, even if they've been out as bi for years (like me), still often find themselves questioning whether they are really bi or bi enough. In my 11 years of being out and interacting with the bi community, I've found that this is probably the most unifying bi experience. The world around us isn't great at recognizing or celebrating bisexuality. Every bi person I know (and I know a lot of them) has been asked at some point in their lives if they're sure they're not 'actually gay' or 'actually straight', based on their dating history. Normally more than once.

As much as I'd love it to, I doubt this book will cause a huge revolution where everyone suddenly understands and celebrates bisexuality. So, if you decide that bi is the right label for you, you're probably going to come across people who don't believe in bisexuality, who tell you that they think you're probably just gay or straight, or flat-out tell you that you'll pick a side eventually.

I wish I could leave everyone who picks up this book with enough confidence in their bisexuality never to let these questions and dismissals get to them, but that's just not possible. Instead, I hope you find it within yourself to validate and feel assured in your bisexuality. Even if you sometimes have doubts. That's okay. We all do.

So, with that in mind, let's have a look at what 'bisexual' actually means.

Attraction to more than one gender

The definition of 'bisexual' most widely used by bi organizations is 'an attraction to more than one gender'. Bisexual activist Robyn Ochs' quote is most often used to expand this definition of bisexuality:

> I call myself bisexual because I acknowledge that I have in myself the potential to be attracted – romantically and/or sexually – to people of more than one sex and/or gender, not necessarily at the same time, not necessarily in the same way, and not necessarily to the same degree. (Ochs 2014b)

This is also the definition of bisexuality that I use because I find it to be the most inclusive and malleable. Some bisexual people are always attracted to certain genders (e.g., men, women, and non-binary people) in the same way and with the same intensity.

Others may be more attracted to certain genders, but less to others. Some are attracted to some genders in a sexual way but are uninterested in pursuing romantic relationships with them and vice versa.

I think this to be the best definition because it provides a welcoming space for anyone who isn't strictly monosexual (attracted to one gender). For example, women who are attracted to women and non-binary people might use this definition as opposed to or even alongside a definition of 'lesbian'. It can encompass agender people who are only attracted to other agender people and people of non-binary gender identities. It can be used by men who have romantic and sexual relationships with women, and only sexual relationships with men.

There are so many different combinations and expressions of bisexuality that can fit under Ochs' description, which is why so many organizations have adopted it. For example, BiNet USA, the oldest bi organization in the world, builds on Ochs' description to define bisexual as:

> A person whose enduring physical, romantic and/or emotional attraction is to other people of various sexes and/or gender identities. Individuals may experience this attraction in differing ways and degrees over their lifetime. (BiNet USA 2016)

This definition is useful because it includes people whose attractions may change and develop over time. For example, someone who was previously only attracted to people whose gender is different from their own (i.e. a man only attracted to women) who falls in love with someone of the same gender and now only feels an attraction to them or same-gender people might call themselves bi to acknowledge the legitimacy of their previous (and possible future) desires, even if they no longer feel that. I often go through prolonged phases of only being interested in

women; when I'm out and about, I catch myself only noticing women, only thinking about women, only looking up the
name of actresses in movies. This will go on until I start having
an identity crisis, wondering if I'm a lesbian who's just been
confused this whole time. It's usually about that time when I'll
lock eyes with a soft-haired man across a cafe, or be introduced
to a friend of a friend with a lot of black-and-white tattoos, and
suddenly remember that men exist. Some people might describe
a person whose attractions change over time as 'fluid', 'queer', or
'abrosexual'. All of these can co-exist with the bi label.

The UK bisexual group The Bisexual Index uses the definition:

> someone who is attracted to more than one gender. You might
> care about the gender of your partner a lot, a little, or not at
> all – but their gender doesn't prevent you from being attracted
> to them. (bisexualindex.org.uk n.d.)

This is useful because it encompasses those who may consider
themselves 'genderblind' (i.e. they don't care at all about the
gender of their objects of desire) and those for whom gender
is an important factor in the multiplicated attraction. On the
Bisexual Resource Center website, Robyn Ochs writes about a
conversation she had with her friend Alberto, who also identifies
as bisexual, and who considers gender expression a crucial factor
in their attraction. Ochs writes:

> 'Regardless of gender? No, no, no! There's no "regardless" about
> it for me. For me it's all about difference. I'm attracted to
> cheerleaders and football players. It's precisely the extremes of
> difference that attract me.' Alberto is attracted to the poles, to
> super-masculine guys and super-feminine girls.
>
> Others are attracted to masculinity and/or femininity, regard-
> less of a person's sex. Some of us who identify as bisexual are in

fact 'gender-blind'. For others—in fact for me—it's androgyny or the blending of genders that compels. (Bisexual Resource Center n.d.-c)

Attracted to similar and different genders

This is a definition that you come across more commonly online, in my experiences at least. People who use this definition tend to do so because they find it to be more inclusive of all genders. Where 'attracted to more than one gender' might imply that there is a quantifiable amount of separate genders the person is attracted to, the 'similar and different' definition allows room for a more fluid approach to attraction.

But, as the bisexual support blog Bi-Privilege.tumblr explains, this definition may not include bisexual people who do not feel attraction to genders similar to their own: 'It is important to remember that bisexuals can be attracted to multiple genders without being attracted to people of their own gender. For example, an agender bi person may be attracted to women, bigender, and genderfluid people, or a bi woman might be attracted to men and agender people' (Bi-Privilege.tumblr n.d.).

Alternatively, bisexual people may also not be attracted to people of different genders. For example, a genderfluid person who may identify between male and agender may be attracted to people of those genders, but not anyone who falls towards the female end of the gender matrix.

Attraction beyond gender

Bi Pride UK, an organization dedicated to ensuring there is bisexual representation in every pride parade in the UK and the organizer of the UK's first Bi Pride event, uses the definition 'attraction beyond gender' in order to be inclusive of everyone who identifies as non-monosexual and uses labels such as bisexual, pansexual, biromantic, panromantic (we'll talk about the difference between romantic and sexual orientations in a bit), queer, sexually fluid, or without labels. The chair of Bi Pride UK, Avi Kay, explained to me over Facebook Messenger what this definition means to the organization:

> For us, we wanted to find a short phrase, shorter than 'attracted to more than one gender' or similar, which would double up as a strapline for us, but also we needed to make sure that it was broad enough so that people who use different labels (whether bi, pan or anything else) felt it described them without parts of the community potentially feeling excluded, and inclusive enough to not focus on romantic attraction to the exclusion of sexual attraction or vice versa.
>
> We recognise within this, that for some people, 'attraction beyond gender' could mean not seeing gender or gender not playing a part in your attraction, which for many people isn't how they experience their identity, but we don't use the phrase to mean this. For us it is a catch-all term, but we don't expect that it will mean the same thing universally.

My favourite part of this explanation is that it acknowledges that no one sentence (or even word) will ever be able to completely capture a group of people who may overlap and intersect in the way that they experience the world, because as similar as those experiences are, they will never be exactly the same. No two multi-gender attracted (MGA) people will ever experience multi-gender attraction in the same way. But as Bi Pride and all other community/activist groups know, that doesn't mean it isn't useful and important to try to bring people together through our shared experiences so we can organize, support, and, perhaps most importantly, find each other.

BI THE WAY

I predominantly use 'bi' and 'queer' to refer to the fact that I'm attracted to people regardless of gender. 'Bisexual' was probably the first label I was aware of for my experiences, back as a teenager in the '90s, so it has history for me. Having said that, it took me years from applying it to myself in my head to actually saying it out loud to others. Another reason I use it is that over the years, I have found community through and around it. I use 'queer' to encompass not just my bisexuality but my other...well, queernesses. As well as bi, I'm on the ace spectrum and I'm some flavour of non-binary. At some point it just gets easier to say, 'I'm queer af'.

dr elmyra

Bisexuality as freedom

To me, the word bisexual sounds like the click of my key in the front door, welcoming me home. It's friendship, community, spending afternoons at BiFest, the stress and elation of helping organize Pride floats. It's the anticipation of sending risky texts, the bitter-sweetness of unrequited crushes, the rush of relief of coming out to accepting friends. It's the hum of my old moped as I drove home from my first boyfriend's house, the taste of rum as I kissed strangers in the Student's Union bar, the smell of my first girlfriend's hair as she fell asleep next to me.

It allows me to be multitudes and contradictions; to be attracted to men but not want to date them, to switch gender as easily as clothes, to be a walking queer cliche as often as I pass. It is an irrefutable cornerstone of who I am, and it allows me to love and be loved in a myriad of ways. No matter what semantic definition I use, it means to be open and proud about my ability to love people of any gender. To me, 'bisexual' means freedom.

Long before I had even started to feel attraction to anyone, poet, essayist, and activist June Jordan had already put this feeling into words. In her essay 'On Bisexuality and Cultural Pluralism', she writes:

> Bisexuality means I am free and I am as likely to want to love a woman as I am likely to want to love a man, and what about that? Isn't that what freedom implies?
>
> If you are free, you are not predictable and you are not controllable. To my mind, that is the keenly positive, politicizing significance of bisexual affirmation...to insist upon the equal validity of all the components of social/sexual complexity. (Jordan 1998)

If you decide that 'bisexual' is the label you want to use, you will eventually find your own definition. It might be one of the ones explained above, or one you choose for yourself. It might change over time, or even regularly. It doesn't have to perfectly sum up your every desire and feeling about love and sex; in fact I don't think any single word or explanation can.

Other labels

Not everyone who experiences multi-gender attraction calls

themselves bi. Labels are highly subjective, and people choose the labels they do for complex, layered reasons. These decisions are influenced by their culture, the community around them, the information and resources they have access to, their political beliefs, and many, many other reasons. What follows are just some of the most common words (other than bisexual) people use to describe their multi-gender attraction.

Pansexual

'Pansexual' is usually defined as 'attraction to all genders', or 'attraction regardless of gender'. The term has been around for several decades but has become increasingly popular in the last few decades, mostly due to the internet facilitating the spread of information and resources about sexuality and identity.

Whilst pansexuality is its own valid identity, it's similarity and overlap with bisexuality has led to a lot of discussion and debate about the difference between the two. In recent years, as more celebrities and public figures have come out as pan – such as Brendon Urie, Lizzo, and Miley Cyrus – many media outlets have run articles that have tried to explain the difference between the two terms by wrongly stating that bisexuality means 'only attracted to men and women' and suggesting that pansexuality is more inclusive and progressive.

Because of this misinformation about bisexuality, some people use pansexual instead of bisexual because they erroneously believe that 'bisexual' means 'only attracted to binary genders' (sometimes people go as far as to say that bisexual people are only attracted to cis men and women; this is deeply transphobic as it implies that trans men/women are not 'real' men/women). As we can see from the definitions of bisexual used by bi organizations, this is not the case at all. As well as this, it has also been claimed that the bisexual community used to define the word as 'attraction to men and women' and that the broadening of the term to include non-binary genders is a contemporary one. This is also easily disproved; the 'Anything that Moves' bisexual manifesto written in 1991, warns against the assumption that bi is binary:

> Bisexuality is a whole, fluid identity. Do not assume that bisexuality is binary or duogamous in nature: that we have 'two' sides or that we must be involved simultaneously with both genders to be fulfilled human beings. In fact, don't assume that there are only two genders.

As we will see in upcoming chapters, the way other people have defined bisexuality and the bi community does not always match the way we have defined and regarded ourselves and there are many sources out there that described bisexuality as binary. This can be said of most queer identities, as queerness itself is often pathologized and othered by non-queer people as they try to study and understand it through a heteronormative lens. In this book, I will only be using the definitions communities have given themselves, because I feel like those are the only ones that really matter.

Because of these misconceptions, some bi people have come to think that identifying as pan is biphobic, as it implies that bi is binary, outdated, or transphobic. A lot has been written on this topic, and a lot of it wrongly accuses all pan people of trying to erase bisexuality. While there are certainly people who identify as pan for biphobic reasons, identifying as pan is not inherently biphobic. In the same way, some bi people do use 'bi' to mean attracted to cis men and women, but this doesn't make identifying as bi inherently transphobic (but those people are).

There are a myriad of reasons someone might identify as

pan instead of bi and lots of people even use both labels, such as Wesley who told me over Twitter; 'I use "bisexual" because people know what it means, because I don't feel a need to cede ground to the biphobia that makes us afraid to say it, and because I like reclaiming a word that was imposed on us by presumably straight scientists. I use "pansexual" because it doesn't hint at a binary (even though that's not what "bi-" has to mean in this case) and because it's a word queer people adopted for themselves rather than one scientists have assigned them as a population to be studied.'

In my mind, the overlap between bi and pan should not be a cause for friction but for celebration; as a community, multi-gender attracted people have come far enough in our journey for acceptance and visibility that we can create multiple words for our similar experiences, desires, and attractions. Instead of having our language limited by lack of access to information and resources about ourselves, we can now create and build our language, taking up space and exploring the beautiful intricacies of our lives, experiences, and communities.

BI THE WAY

I use bisexual and queer. For a long time I felt really uncomfortable thinking of myself as part of the queer community since I'm married to a guy I met soon after coming out. Calling myself queer even when I don't 'look' queer is a way I've found to claim for space for boring queer people like myself and make it very, very clear in many of the 'straight' places that ppl in the closet can count on me and that straight ppl need to check themselves. I used to really, really hate on myself about whether I'm bi or pan. I'm pretty whatever about bodies and gender, but people do not understand what pan is and I don't want to constant-ly explain. I had a bit of a 'Galaxy brain' realization that everyone I am attracted to on the gender spectrum falls pretty neatly in one of two general personalities. No one really knows that I've come to that realization, but it does give me a small amount of personal pleasure whenever I tell someone I'm bisexual.

Sidney Van Wyk Lee

Omni/polysexual

Both omnisexual and polysexual are words for people attracted to multiple/all genders. Omni is often described as 'someone who notices their partner's gender, but doesn't care', whereas poly comes from the Greek prefix *poly-*, meaning many.

Fluid

Someone with a fluid orientation refers to someone whose sexual and/or romantic attraction changes over time or regularly.

Queer

Although not everyone who identifies as queer is multi-gender attracted, lots of people who use the umbrella term are. Queer was originally used as a pejorative to refer to same-sex couples, but over time the word has been (mostly) reclaimed, although some people still reject the use of the term.

Most of the reclamation work was done by radical black activists in the late '80s and early '90s; these groups used the word to distinguish themselves from the white middle-class LGBTQIA+ movement. It became an important part of AIDS activism, particularly used by groups like Queer Nation and ACT UP.

BI THE WAY

Personally, I use the labels bisexual and queer! I use bisexual a lot because I spent so many years denying myself from labelling myself as bisexual and now I never shut up about it and it's liberating! I don't personally use pansexual because I only heard the term after I came out as bisexual. I don't mind being labelled as it, I just don't use it personally. I have really embraced queer and use it a ton. I feel like as a person of colour, I'm a little distant from the 'mainstream' scene, so to speak, which is often very white dominated. Using queer in the context of being a queer person of colour allows me to feel connected to that side of the community, that shared experience. Queer feels very 'not of the ordinary' in its definition, something that resonates strongly with me.

Vaneet Mehta

The word became popular due to its vague, encompassing, and inclusive nature. Queer doesn't just mean gay; it's an expression of freedom from cisheteronormativity. 'It's an umbrella term used to define a spectrum of marginalised identities ranging from cis white gay men to asexual non-binary black individuals,' wrote Journalist Jake Hall for *Dazed* in 2016. Queer is everything that opposes the hegemonic norm, heteronormativity, cisnormativity, the ways we are expected to love and lust.

The meaning and history of 'queer' is so rich, fluid, turbulent, contradictory, empowering, hurtful, and nebulous that it would take an entire book to explore, not just a subsection of one chapter. Luckily, *a lot* of people have written *a lot* of books about queerness, queer theory, and queer lives. I encourage you to go out and read them, read blogs, watch videos, talk to queer people – especially queer elders – and explore what the word means to you. Does it make you feel empowered, or shrink away? Does it capture the amorphous nature of your identity, or does it make it feel less solid and real? There are no right or wrong answers, as long as you're not telling anyone else how they should feel about it.

For me, I love the word and use it interchangeably with 'bi' to describe myself. I see it as one of my community labels. Like a lot of bi people, I don't always feel a part of or welcome in LGBTQIA+ communities (we'll talk about that in a few chapters), but I feel more welcome in queer communities, which are often more accepting of fluid, vague, and undefined identities.

In this book, I'll be using 'queer' interchangeably with 'LGBT-QIA+' (unless stated otherwise), and as a way to refer to everyone who doesn't fit the allosexual, alloromantic, heterosexual, cis-gender standard we're all expected to fit.

Wait, allosexual and alloromantic?
What the hell does that mean?

Asexual refers to anyone who doesn't experience sexual attraction, and aromantic covers a lack of romantic attraction. Allosexual and alloromantic, then, are the opposite. As queer communities begin to come out of the shadows due to more tolerance in society and greater connection and access to information thanks to cheaper printing and, of course, the internet, new words and labels for sexual and romantic desires and identities have proliferated and will continue to do so. This is especially true online, in spaces where young people congregate, such as Tumblr and Twitter.

Some people deride these so-called 'micro-identities' as unnecessary or even harmful as they 'dilute' other communities or pathologize universal human experiences. While I take these criticisms onboard, I see these new words as tools of empowerment, allowing people to find connections with others who have experiences similar to theirs and to better communicate their feelings and selves.

BI THE WAY

Publicly, I refer to myself as bisexual and queer. I initially identified as lesbian and it took me a lot of years after falling in love with and marrying an AMAB (announced male at birth) person to feel comfortable in the queer community again. So I like to embrace queer as an umbrella term, and work on fighting biphobia by claiming bi. Casually, I still use gay as an umbrella term because growing up everything was 'gay'. At home, my partner and I are polyamorous and genderqueer/gender fluid/gender is a social construct and also exhausting. Neither of us has taken steps toward any sort of medical transition, in part because it's expensive, and in part because it's not like identifying as the opposite gender is any more correct than the ones we were assigned at birth.

Dr Corinne Tagliarina

Romantic vs sexual orientations

The types of words and identifiers that tend to receive the most flak are those that separate romantic from sexual attraction. Most people just use one label to cover their entire orientation, because they only want to have romantic relationships with the people they are sexually attracted to, and vice versa. For most people, even though 'bi' denotes 'bi*sexual*' the word is still sufficient to cover their entire orientation.

But for others, there is still a disconnect between their romantic and sexual orientations. For example, someone might identify as bi ace, meaning they're open to romantic/emotional relationships with people of different genders, but not sexually attracted to anyone (ace is slang for asexual). Or, someone might identify as a pan aro, meaning they're sexually attracted to people of any gender, but don't experience a desire for romantic relationships with anyone (aro is slang for aromantic).

A lot of people have trouble imagining how someone might be interested in a relationship without also wanting to have sex with their partners, as we're bombarded with messages and media telling us that sex is the ultimate expression within a relationship. This runs so deep in our society that it has even been enshrined in law. Under Section 12 of the Matrimonial Causes Act 1973, refusal or inability to consummate a marriage is grounds for annulment in England and Wales. This only applies to opposite-sex marriages; the Marriage (Same Sex Couples) Act 2013 specifically excludes failure to consummate as grounds for annulment. This has as much do with what is legally recognized as sex as it does with the validity of sexless marriages, but it is a good example of how intertwined our cisheteronormative (assuming straight and cis is the standard) society sees love, sex, and reproductions as being. For that reason, a lot of people find it useful to define their sexual and romantic orientation if they happen to differ.

'My sexual and romantic identities don't align and so I use different labels to describe them. This isn't uncommon. While we often talk about sexualities, romantic attraction is actually quite different. Some people can be sexually attracted to certain

types of people or genders but experience romantic attraction to different types of people or genders. I'm bisexual and
demiromantic and this confuses a lot of people. It means that I
experience a huge amount of stereotyping,' activist and editor in
chief of *Stand Up* Magazine Steph Famsworth explained to me.

> Demiromantic simply means that I don't experience romantic
> attraction and will only ever experience it after forming an
> intense emotional connection with someone. That is quite
> different to alloromantic experiences, because people generally
> do experience a bit of romantic attraction quite regularly. That
> doesn't mean love. It often takes a lot for people to fall in love.
> Romantic attraction is a scale with love being at one end. But the
> scale includes a lot of other expressions of romantic attraction
> too such as wanting to date, wanting to hold hands, wanting
> to explore romantic possibilities with a person. I don't want
> any of that with anyone. And that's quite different to the way
> I experience my bisexuality, which is just as important to me.

It's important to note that being asexual doesn't necessarily mean
being celibate. Lots of asexual people still enjoy the physical
sensations of sex and petting with their romantic partners, in
the same way you don't need to be attracted to a masseuse to
enjoy being touched by them and find a massage satisfying.

Identity vs behaviour

Some people behave in ways that we consider bisexual while
not actually using that label. I'm not talking about cuffing
their jeans and tucking in their shirt (if that makes no sense to
you, sorry that you were born before 1995; but don't worry, we'll

discuss online bi culture in a few chapters' time), rather, they may engage in intimate relationships with people of different genders while still (publicly, at least) referring to themselves as monosexual.

This is known as being 'behaviourally bisexual' and is a term mainly used in academia, when it's important to differentiate people by who they sleep with, regardless of how they identify. For example, when studying aspects related to sexual health, it may be useful to highlight men who sleep with people of different genders while still calling themselves straight, as these men will have different sexual health needs and experiences.

It is unfortunately common, especially among men, for people who are multi-gender attracted to call themselves straight, even if they are acting on their desires. This is because same-gender attraction, and bisexuality in particular, is still highly stigmatized.

In this book, I'll be talking exclusively about people who identify as bisexual, even if they're not 'behaviourally bisexual'. After all, one of the key aims of this book is to make people realize that the only thing you need to do to be bi is to say 'Yes, I am bi!' – even if you have to whisper it – because there is no right or wrong way to be bi.

I also don't find the term 'behaviourally bisexual' very useful, because there is a myriad of reasons why a monosexual person may engage in intimate/sexual experiences with people of multiple genders, from sex work to internalized homophobia. It also suggests that there is a certain way of conducting yourself that counts as bisexual, i.e. engaging in sexual experiences with people of multiple genders. In my view, this delegitimizes other bi experiences such as being in a monogamous long-term relationship whilst still fantasizing about and desiring people of different genders or choosing to be celibate whilst still acknowledging your bisexual desires. People know themselves better than anyone else does, and we should respect the labels people choose for themselves, even if we don't agree that they fit them. Later in this book I will be discussing people who are multi-gender attracted but don't call themselves bi, but I will be doing so through the lens of being closeted or struggling with internalized biphobia. But even then, I won't be concluding that those people should come out as bi if it doesn't feel right to them.

The American Institute of Bisexuality and its publication bi.org use the 'AIB model', suggesting that a person's orientation is made up of attraction, identity, and behaviour. They explain (on bi.org) that attraction refers to 'a person's capacity for sexual and/or romantic feelings. It is the single most important factor in determining an individual's sexual orientation'; identity covers 'the ways a person thinks about themselves as well as the way they wish to be seen by others', and behaviour indicates 'how a person interacts with others romantically or sexually. It's important to note that behavior does not necessarily always reflect attraction or identity' (Bi.org n.d.-b). They go on to explain:

> For most people, attraction is the single most important factor in determining sexual orientation. While we may choose how we behave and how we identify, we have little choice in deciding whom we find attractive. (Bi.org n.d.-b)

So, are you bi?

Hopefully now you have some more information about bisexuality and other multi-gender attraction labels and you can start to think about what kind of attraction(s) – if any – you experience and what words feel right to you. Presumably if you've picked up this book, 'bi' is at least in the running. It's important to remember that labels are not the be all and end all. They are useful as a way of finding people like us and organizing around issues that people face, but the world won't end if you never decide on a label that fits you best.

If you decide you want to label your orientation, here's an exercise that might help: in a safe and private space say the words 'I am bi' to yourself. Then, 'I am pan', 'I am gay/a lesbian', 'I am ace'. Think about how each of those makes you feel. Does anything click inside you? It's okay if it doesn't. It can take years to find the right label for you. These phrases are still considered taboo and, for many of us, the only times we say them are when we are coming out. This means they can become loaded with feelings of anxiety. Allowing yourself to say them, to take away some of their exceptionalism, to let them become a more common and mundane part of your vocabulary, may help you figure out which one feels most like home to you.

Think about what each means and how that lines up with your experiences and desires. Remember that these words are pins, not tattoos; you can take them off whenever you want. You can wear multiple, or none, or swap them regularly. You can use some around family and co-workers, and others around friends and partners. You may change them hundreds of times during your life. Labels are supposed to be a tool to empower us, not a stick to beat each other with, and certainly not a box that we have to put ourselves in and never leave.

CHAPTER 2

What If I Have a Preference?

There's no right or wrong way to be bi, but unfortunately there *is* a common misconception that being bi means being equally attracted to men and women. This leads to the idea that someone is actually gay or straight if they are more attracted to or date one gender more often.

As humans we love to put things into categories and from an evolutionary standpoint it's fared us pretty well; if you see an animal you don't recognize that's white with black stripes, big paws, big teeth, and looks like a cat, it's pretty useful to put it into the category of 'tiger', even if it doesn't fit the usual description of 'orange with black stripes'. In Western thinking, we also tend to do our categorical world-building in binaries: safe/dangerous, edible/poisonous, good/bad, male/female, straight/gay, etc., and because Western thinking has been exported globally via colonialism, these less-than-helpful binaries have taken root around the world (we'll discuss this in more depth in the next chapter).

Ultimately, the way we categorize something boils down to a single binary: is vs is not. If something does not fit the category of 'tiger', then regardless of what it might be, it is not a tiger, right? But what about a liger (a tiger crossed with a lion)? A liger fits both the categories of 'a tiger' and 'not a tiger'. It becomes its own category. The same can be said about a platypus, which is both a land mammal and aquatic fowl. By being both those things, it becomes neither.

It makes us uncomfortable when things don't fit into our existing categories and binaries. It challenges us to think about the world in a more fluid and complex way. It means we have to take a step back from the catalogue of information we have about what something is and how we interact with it before we make a decision on how to proceed. This pause can be the difference between life and death (oh look, another binary) when trying to work out if a liger counts as a tiger, but it's generally a good thing when it encourages us to think outside of the usual ways we treat and interact with people who fit into certain categories.

One of the main issues people have with bisexuals is that we don't neatly fit in the dominant categories of gay or straight. Especially if we're doing something that supposedly makes us look gay or straight, like dating someone of a similar or different gender, but still refuse to be put in one of those categories, we challenge people's worldview about sexuality. When people ask me and other bi people – which they do a lot – what gender we prefer or have had more relationships with, what they're actually asking is 'Which are you? Basically gay or basically straight?' But no matter any preference we might have, no bi person is 'basically gay' or 'basically straight'. They're just bi.

Bisexuality is a spectrum. Well, a spectrum implies that there are only two end points, but as there are more than two genders, bisexuality is more like a matrix or a big, messy chess board. Some people move around the board in all different directions throughout their lives, some only move in one direction, and some don't move at all. All of these different players and pieces make up the rich and varied landscape of the bi community.

BI THE WAY

I'm bisexual and am attracted stronger to women than men and prefer dating women (for various reasons), but I have dated more men. I am also attracted to men more often, although less strongly than to women. I think one big reason is that it is easier and more likely for me to find a male partner because the number of queer women around me is lower than the number of men attracted to women. And I am also cautious of dating queer women because I had to endure some really biphobic comments from the queer community.

Anonymous

While there's no research into bi people's preferences (which is probably a good thing, because people would just use this data as a way to deny that bisexuality is real), it seems to be pretty common for bi people to have them. Online, it's not unusual to come across jokes about bi girls liking all girls and maybe one or two boys. These posts tend to go something like: 'Being bisexual means I'm attracted to every girl I've ever seen and the Sprouse twins only' or 'I'm bi, which means I like every type of girl and boys who wear eyeliner'. Okay, enough of me subtly telling you my preferences (Cole Sprouse, if you're reading this, DM me). While these might be an attempt to feel 'gay enough', often a preference for women is a way for us to distance ourselves from misogyny and heteronormative gender roles.

'I realized that in our society women are grateful when a man behaves in a sensitive manner, but expect sensitivity of a woman as a matter of course. I decided that I would not settle for less from men, realizing that it means that I may be categorically eliminating most men as potential partners. So be it,' explains iconic bi activist Robyn Ochs (2014a) in an essay called 'Bisexuality, Feminism, Men and Me', where she explores her journey of unlearning compulsory heterosexuality, and holding men and women to the same standards when it comes to relationships and attraction, after a lifetime of believing she must settle for a man.

The term 'compulsory heterosexuality', which was first coined by Adrienne Rich, an American poet, essayist, and feminist in her 1982 essay 'Compulsory Heterosexuality and Lesbian Existence', is often invoked to discuss the belief that many queer women have that they must or inevitably will end up with a man eventually. The phrase refers to the way in which relationships between a man and a woman are considered obligatory and the only natural/acceptable forms of relationships. Rich believes that mainstream society uses media, art, and pop culture to reinforce this message and convince women that we are only attracted to men. In her interview with gay actress and comedian Cameron Esposito on Cameron's podcast *Queery*, bisexual YouTuber and author Gaby Dunn discusses her experiences with compulsory heterosexuality:

I am bisexual, I've been in love with men, I've dated men but in this economy I can't imagine going home to a dude... But I was looking back on the past and I was wondering how many relationships or encounters I've had with men where it was just me being like, 'I admire you and I think you're cool and funny,' and I've been confused by movies and music and everything in our society to believe that the next step here is we have sex. [But with women] there's nothing telling me that the next step in a female friendship is that we [have sex].

This is definitely something I can relate to and I imagine a lot of other bi women can too. Looking back over the many 'crushes' I've had on boys, I've realized that not a small number of them were in fact strong feelings of admiration, a coveting of qualities they had and I wanted, a friendship crush, a deep appreciation of their looks/aesthetic, a desire for platonic physical affection, or even just good old-fashioned male validation (which, as women, we're taught is the only type that matters).

Whilst the concept of compulsory heterosexuality has been very useful for many queer women, particularly lesbians and asexual women, it is often weaponized against bi/pan women as a way of shaming us for being attracted to men. 'Bi women are just lesbians who can't get over compulsory heterosexuality and can't fully come out because they don't want to give up the benefits of heterosexuality', the claim often goes. While bi women do experience compulsory heterosexuality, claiming all bi women are just struggling with compulsory heterosexuality is deeply biphobic and invalidating. Once again, it's an attempt to put bi people into the domain binary of gay and straight, based on their preferences or even people's projections of their preferences. There are lots of reasons why a bi women may prefer women and/or not to date men, and claiming that these women must be lesbian instead of bi derails valid and necessary conversations about preferences, experiencing sexism as a queer woman, and the overlap between bi+ and lesbian identities and experiences.

In 2017 I attended my first ever BiFest in London, a one-day festival dedicated to celebrating bisexuality, and I remember the frustration of one woman as she explained in a safer space session how often she gets called a lesbian and told it doesn't matter if she's actually bi because she is married to a woman. As she explained, no one ever calls her wife (a lesbian) bisexual and then insists her real identity doesn't matter, so why do they keep doing it to her? Similarly, I wrote about all of this in 2018 for bi.org, in an article called 'Dear Lesbians, No, I'm Not Gay' (Shearing 2018a), which was sparked by the amount of memes I'd seen at the time about bisexual women fancying all women and a small amount of men, and the multiple responses telling the poster that they were just a lesbian who isn't able to overcome compulsory heterosexuality. It's been one of the most shared and engaged with articles I've written to date, which suggests to me that being a bi woman with a preference for women, and being frustrated at having your identity erased because of it, is a pretty common experience. I concluded in the article (if you can't quote your own articles in your own books, why bother writing either?):

> Thanks to monosexism, the harmful idea that only monosexual (straight or gay) identities are real, valid, or stable, many bi people struggle with thinking they must actually be gay when they realise they are same-gender attracted. It's not uncommon for bi women to identify as a lesbian when they first come out, before accepting that their attractions to men are still genuine. Perpetuating the idea that bi women are wrong about their identity if they shy away from attraction to men perpetuates this stereotype and further marginalises bi women. Believing that a woman must 'really be a lesbian' if she has a strong pref-erence for women creates an environment where there is only one way to be bi; to be equally into men and women. This erases and minimizes a whole host of bi expressions, including those from bi women who don't like men at all, bi women who have

experienced trauma from men that has affected their sexuality, and bi women who are just choosing to not deal with the sexism that can come with dating men.

Of course, it isn't just women who experience this. Men and non-binary people often have their bisexuality erased or invalidated if they have a preference. Bisexual activist and writer Zachary Zane says he has a preference for dating men, not just because he finds them more attractive but because he finds it difficult to date women with his 'very gay lifestyle' and because he struggles with having his queerness erased when he's in a different-gender relationship. 'All of the factors that influence my preference are cultural and societal. And if we lived in a world without misogyny, biphobia, homophobia, and restrictive gender norms, I don't think I would have a preference as to whom I date,' he writes for bi.org (Zane 2018). 'But this is the real world we live in, and while I want to do my best to change the world to make it less sexist, biphobic, etc., I don't need to take a stand in my romantic life. Dating is tough enough as is. I don't want to take on additional challenges because society is screwed up.'

BI THE WAY

I was raised Catholic and attended religious schools through college. I wasn't explicitly told homosexuality was a sin, it just wasn't discussed. I didn't know bisexuality was real until college, when I met one – one – person who identified that way. Then my brother came out, and while I wondered if there might be something within me too I hadn't quite figured it out. Plus, I had to deal with my parents, who were reeling, and asking me all sorts of questions, through my young adulthood. I married a man I had met when I was 19, so didn't sexually explore much. When our marriage got tough I started considering other people and that's when I finally acknowledged my bisexuality. I was 35. From there it was an uphill battle to get my husband to accept it (he thought I was straight) and my brother (classic pit-stop mentality). But in looking back I realized that all my really intense feelings were for girls or women. I just thought I was a really good friend! But in reality, I was probably in love with some of them. Now that I'm self-aware, I recognize that I'm mainly into women, and it's kind of a fluke that I wound up married to a man, whom I love, but it's a different relationship.

Anonymous

What if my dating history doesn't match my preference?

To make things more complicated – or rather, more rich and interesting – it isn't uncommon for bi people's dating history to be completely unmatched to their preference. Many of the women I spoke to who have a preference for women had either dated more or only men. For most, this came down to a few key reasons.

First, there are more straight people than there are LGB people. While the amount of openly queer people is on the rise, we are still pretty outnumbered. The latest stats (2018) at the time of writing from America suggest that 4.5 per cent of the population identify as not straight, while here in the UK that number is 2 per cent (latest statistics from 2017 at the time of writing). Which means that you're far more likely to meet someone of a different gender who's attracted to you than you are someone of a similar gender. This makes it much harder for queer people to find other queer people to date, and it may explain why so many bi women have had more relationships with men, even if they prefer other genders.

The second is a good ol' fashioned fear of girls. While straight male pop-punk singers like to pretend they have a monopoly on not being able to talk to women, it's an experience that really belongs to queer girls. In fact, not being able to flirt, talk to girls, or even tell if a girl is interested has become a prolific meme among young queer girls online. This is known as the 'useless lesbian' trope, although it applies to all queer women. Culturally speaking, there's a deeply ingrained script of how romantic or sexual relationships form between men and women. If the majority of media is to be believed, all relationships between men and women start like this:

- A man meets a woman and begins pursuing her. The woman is uninterested/hesitant at first, to show that she's not 'easy', but eventually his persistence is rewarded by her relenting, and the two fall in love/date/sleep together. Some examples of this in the media include *Aladdin*, *When Harry Met Sally*, *Sixteen Candles*, *Notting Hill*, *Grease*, *Jane Eyre*, Ross and Rachel in *Friends*.

- Two friends realize that they have been 'more than friends' the entire time and, after some miscommunication, start a relationship. Think *Always Be My Maybe*, *Friends with Benefits*, *Clueless*, *One Day*, Monica and Chandler in *Friends*.

Obviously, this isn't how most relationships start, and, in fact, the first is based on the objectification of women as a prize to be 'won' by men. But these cultural narratives are a key mechanism of upholding compulsory heterosexuality and leading women to overstate their interest in men and repressing their interest in women. After all, there is no cultural script for women pursuing women, men pursuing men, or non-binary people pursuing or being pursued by anyone. In one way, this gives us an amazing opportunity to write our own stories and create our own versions of romance and desire in ways that are healthier and more fulfilling than the 'boy meets girl' narrative. On the flip side, it also means lots of queer people – especially young queer people – struggle to explore their desires because, well, we just have no idea how to do it.

Fear of facing homophobia/biphobia is another factor that can keep people from exploring their preferences. We'll explore this in *a lot* more depth in the chapter on biphobia, but feeling uncomfortable going to or being in queer spaces makes it very difficult to meet potential partners of the same gender. The final factor is the somewhat bitter-sweet serendipity of meeting your long-term, monogamous partner before you've had the chance to really explore your identity. A lot of the Boomers and Gen Xers I spoke to about their preferences not matching their dating histories cited this cause, because it used to be much more common to marry young.

BI THE WAY

So I'm a 35-year-old bi woman. I met my husband in middle school. We started dating freshman year of high school. I didn't realize I was bi until I was in college. In high school I had a big questioning of my sexuality. My family wasn't (and still isn't) accepting of the LGBTQ+ community. I didn't want to lose them and had a long-time boyfriend in high school, so I didn't see the point in talking to them about it. I came out to my then fiancé (now husband) when we were living together in college. Fast forward a decade, I'm out to a few select members of my husband's family, a few close friends, and that's it.

Jen Champney

Do I count as bi if I prefer 'the opposite' gender?

Yes!

Even if your attraction is one part same/similar genders to ninety-nine parts different genders, you can still identify as bi if you want to! Because you are. Also, as I hope this book will help you realize, there isn't really such a thing as 'opposite genders' because gender is a matrix as complex and varied as sexuality.

But there are relationships that might look 'straight', and bi people enjoying or even preferring these types of relationships can cause quite a stir in LGBTQIA+ circles. As I write this, there is currently a 'debate' raging on Twitter as to whether bi women deserve to feel uncomfortable at Pride/in queer spaces if they prefer or only date men. Not only is this needlessly mean and unproductive, it also reduces queer women and all our experiences and desires to whom we happen to be dating. It is outright misogynistic to define a woman by her relationship to men, especially if you do so to minimize her queerness and identity. Unfortunately though, the idea that bi people who prefer different-gendered people are posers or a threat to the queer community is depressingly common.

Some people – and I've seen this very acutely from young people online – position themselves as label prescriptivists:

telling others how they should really identify based on whatever information they have on that person's sexuality. This might take the form of telling a bi girl who is wary of dating men that she should actually identify as a lesbian, or telling someone with a preference for different genders that they're really straight. These label cops are also fond of telling bi people that they should actually identify as pan if they like multiple genders, because 'bi' only means two. To that I ask, should August be renamed October because it's actually the eighth month? It's also very common for the prescriptivists to tell lesbians who very occasionally find a man attractive that they're not real lesbians.

I prefer to take a descriptivist approach to labels: one that acknowledges that sexuality is actually unique to every person and that the words we use are just a quick shorthand to help us find people whose identity is similar to ours. I've found this approach to be much more rewarding in allowing others to open up to me and share their experiences, rather than shutting them down and telling them who I think they actually are. I hope that by the end of this book, you'll think so too.

On that note, when I reached out online to talk to bi/pan people about their gender preferences, I was overwhelmed with responses about same-gender preferences and received very few about different-gender preferences. It could be possible that there are fewer bi people with a different-gender preference, but I suspect what is more likely is that multi-gender attracted people who only feel a little bit attracted to same-gender people are less likely to consider themselves bi.

BI THE WAY

I'm a bi mostly-guy married to a pan woman. We're mono-gamous. I never dated a guy because I didn't know I was bi until my 20s and at that point I was already with my current partner. If I'm honest, though, even if I weren't monogamously married, I still might not date men, because it's not a 50/50 split (I'm more often attracted to women) and I also still might be afraid to be visibly queer because of the old shame of internalized homophobia which the current hate-crime-ridden climate exacerbates. I have a fair amount of guilt about that, despite being out to anyone who cares to investigate, and that guilt I think does make me feel less than at-home in queer spaces. I definitely feel 'not queer enough' even though no one I've actually met has ever implied such a thing. And despite having plenty of queer friends (and a queer spouse!), I somehow still feel more like I'm queer-adjacent and hesitate to consider myself 'fully' queer until, I don't know, I'm unafraid and unashamed – which I realize is complete and total BS since I would never hold any other queer person to such a standard.

Anonymous

People who acknowledge that they are not-completely-straight-but-don't-identify-as-bi fall kind of between these categories. Maybe they haven't acted on their same-gender desire with another person, but it's still an important aspect to their identity. This can be a very different experience to people who engage romantically/sexually with people of multi-genders but refuse to call themselves anything other than straight. In their fantastic book *Life Isn't Binary* (2019), authors Meg-John Barker and Alex Iantaffi invite us to think about the differences between desires and identities and who we consider part of 'the bi community'. As they explain:

The most recent national surveys using [a spectrum model of sexuality] have found that nearly half of young people see themselves as somewhere between heterosexual and homosexual, compared to around 2 to 3 percent who actually identify as bisexual. The difference between identity and attraction could very well be the difference between a small minority and a majority. (p.30)

So, someone who might consider themselves a two on a scale where zero is 'only attracted to different genders' and six means 'only attracted to the same gender' (commonly known as the Kinsey scale) might not call themselves bi or pan, even though they have very similar experiences to people who adopt those labels. This has a big impact on how we tell the stories of the bi community, for example when producing statistics about our experiences. It's also important to explore the internal and external factors that might deter someone who falls between a two and a five on the Kinsey scale from identifying as bi.

In order to help people explore why they do or don't use the labels bi or pan if they experience some forms of multi-gender attraction, activist Heron Greenesmith suggests this quick exercise of asking yourself why you don't identify as bi, if you've ever found any member or a different gender attractive (which can be sexual, aesthetically, romantically, or emotionally), if you've ever found someone of a similar gender attractive in any way, or if you've ever found anyone who is non-binary or agender attractive.

Heron makes it clear that the point of exercise is not to suggest that everyone is bi, but rather to encourage people to think about their attractions and why they might have an aversion to the word 'bisexual' (or pansexual, or biromantic, etc.).

BI THE WAY

I've dated men before and still sometimes sleep with them, so claiming bisexuality is honoring that part of myself. Also, bi Tumblr straight up saved my life in my late teens/early 20s and I could never turn away from that. But I've never been that attracted to men I don't think. For ages I thought I was a late bloomer because I had almost no sexual interest in men until I was 19 or so, but I'd been into women since I was 13 years old, I just didn't recognize it like that. So when a man actually captures and holds my attention it's a rare event. But honestly if I never wanted to go near another man again I'd still be bi cause all my longer-term partners (barring my first boyfriend) have been non-binary so lesbian would not work at all. Bi leaves room for complication whilst still having a coherent community in a way that a lot of other labels don't, at least for me.

Maz Hedgehog

Why do non-bi people have such a hard time accepting this?
As we explored earlier, we tend to put people into binary categories as a way to quickly distinguish if someone is safe, or 'one of us'. When something challenges our pre-existing binaries, it can make us uncomfortable and we may defensively try to put that thing or person into a category.

'I think it can feel edgy and threatening precisely because – on some level – it feels like binary categories keep us safe. Holding the understanding that all people have the capacity to be both helpful and harmful to us makes relationships way harder to navigate than if we could divide the world into good and bad people (who should we relate to? in what ways?). Similarly, it is simpler to go after things in life that feel good, and avoid things that feel bad, instead of acknowledging that it's this very pattern that underpins many addictions and other mental health struggles,' Meg-John Barker explains to me over email, after I asked them why having our binaries challenged makes us so uncomfortable.

'This at least partially explains why people who challenge and question binaries like gay/straight or man/woman are viewed with great suspicion in our culture – often assumed to be lying, confused, or immature, for example. If we recognise that sexuality and gender aren't binary, what binaries might we have to challenge next?' they continue.

Many people have suggested using a scale like the Kinsey scale to conceptualize sexuality instead. Unfortunately, because binaries are so intrinsic to how we consider sexuality, a lot of people use the Kinsey or other scales as a gradient between gay and straight. By doing so, they assume that as someone's different-gender attraction decreases, their same-gender attraction increases and vice versa. But as we've seen, this isn't necessarily the case. For example, a bi man who used to prefer women may find his attraction to them waning over time, without wanting to seek out or have more frequent relationships with men. On top of this, where would a non-binary person who is more sexually attracted to men but prefers to have romantic relationships with other non-binary people be placed on the Kinsey scale? Or an asexual, biromantic person? As Terri Clark, sexuality educator and activist, points out in an article for the *National Resource Center on LGBT Aging*:

Kinsey's model is useful in some ways but limited in others because it considers only behavior, not feelings. People can have sexual and erotic feelings and not act on them, or they can participate in sexual behaviors without accompanying erotic feelings. Also Kinsey's scale did not measure attraction over time. Plus behavior alone is not a good indicator of sexual orientation, especially in any one moment.

Several thinkers, sexologists, activists, etc. have proposed different models for thinking about sexuality in ways that don't rely on binaries, including:

- **Sexual configuration theory** – which explores sexuality as a kind of Rubik's Cube with almost infinite combinations of preferences, behaviours, and identities such as gender preferences, being submissive or dominant, romantic preferences, number of partners, etc. Check out Meg-John Barker, Alex Iantaffi, Sari Van Anders, and Julia Scheele's zine 'Mapping Your Sexuality' (2020) to explore your sexual configuration. You can download it online for free.

- **Sexual fluidity** – this theory sort of sees sexuality and desire as a series of behaviours and actions that can change and differ, and have no solid 'sexual identity' behind them.

- **Klein Sexual Orientation Grid** – like sexual configuration theory, this maps sexuality as multi-dimensional, considering emotional bonds, fantasies, and social preferences as being as integral to our sexuality and gender.

It's a lot to take in, right? And there are so many theories about sexuality out there, it would be impossible to list them all. I encourage you to go out and look for some, read about them, and develop in your own mind an approach to sexuality that makes the most sense to you.

So now that we've explored how bisexuality is seen as breaking down one binary, even if someone has a preference, let's discuss why it's accused of upholding another.

CHAPTER 3

Does Bisexuality Reinforce the Gender Binary?

S hort answer: no.

But let's get into the long answer. Which is still no, but let's at least look at why people think it does.

As we explored in the last chapter, in Western culture, we love to put things in binaries, and there's no better example of this than the gender binary. The gender binary is reinforced in our minds from the moment we are born. After all, one of the first things that is imposed on us as soon as we exit the womb is whether we're a boy or a girl. Thanks to modern ultrasounds, a lot of us haven't even drawn our first breath before we're assigned male or female. From there we're given a colour, either blue or pink, so strangers can know what genitals we have, and assumptions about our desires, personalities, likes, dislikes, future partners, and abilities are applied to us. All before we've learned to speak or mastered solid foods.

So what the fuck is gender? As you may have already gathered, I don't think it has all that much to do with what type of squishy bits we have, and most modern scholars agree. Unfortunately, there isn't a succinct or universal agreement of what gender actually is. The *Oxford English Dictionary* returns the definition:

> 1. Either of the two sexes (male and female), especially when considered with reference to social and cultural differences rather than biological ones. The term is also used more broadly to denote a range of identities that do not correspond to established ideas of male and female.
>
> *'a condition that affects people of both genders'*
>
> 1.1 Members of a particular gender considered as a group.
>
> *'social interaction between the genders'*
>
> 1.2 The fact or condition of belonging to or identifying with a particular gender.
>
> *'video ads will target users based only on age and gender'*

But the *Oxford English Dictionary* still defines 'bisexual' as 'sexually attracted not exclusively to people of one particular gender; attracted to both men and women', which as we know from Chapter 1 is not how any bi+ organizations define it. So let's chip off their definition of gender, too.

Alex and Meg-John explain gender in their book *Life Isn't Binary* (2019) as 'a complex biopsychosocial construct', explaining that 'there are biological, psychological, and social components of gender, which are in relationship and which interact with one another in complex ways' (p.58). What that means is that gender is a complex web of different factors: our biology playing one part (but not as much as most people believe), thoughts and feelings playing another, and the context in which we live and grow up yet another. The gender binary is a distinctly Western invention and was exported and violently imposed on the rest of the world through colonialism. Many indigenous cultures have their own gender system and I encourage you to read about these in order to gain a better understanding of how gender is a function of ethnicity and culture as well as biology and psychology. A few resources to check out include:

- QueerAsia.com
- Native Out
- GenderTrust.org.uk
- www.pbs.org/independentlens/content/two-spirits_map – a great interactive map that explores different gender identities around the world
- *Women with Mustaches and Men without Beards: Gender and Sexual Anxieties of Iranian Modernity* by Afsaneh Najmabadi
- *Same-Sex Love in India: Readings from Literature and History* by Ruth Vanita
- *After Eunuchs: Science, Medicine, and the Transformation of Sex in Modern China* by Howard Chiang

But, back to our Western gender binary and how it's imposed on all of us.

As activist and writer Morgan Lev Edward Holleb explains in their book *The A–Z of Gender and Sexuality*:

Gender is performative, but it is not just a performance. Empathizing the performative aspect of gender is reductive, and does not leave room for exploring why certain roles are more comfortable or natural. ...simply saying that 'all gender is performative'... implies that gender is somehow not real. But of course it is real.

It is elusive but extremely material, with concrete consequences. (Holleb 2019, p.126)

The (Latin) root of the issue

So if gender is such a nebulous concept, divorced from our genitals, it's much easier to understand that there are far more than just two genders. As we've seen from the definitions in Chapter 1, bisexuality and the bi community embrace this (well, a large part of it does; I don't want to downplay the trans/non-binaryphobia that definitely exists in the bi community). Yet many people, especially more progressive people and other members of the queer community, still claim that bisexuality implies that there are only two genders...because the prefix bi- means two.

Yes, that's really why.

I have several friends who are bilingual. Their being bilingual does not imply that there are only two languages. As bisexual activist Marcus Morgan (2017) often points out: 'if you hear "Bisexual Visibility Day is September 23rd" & don't angrily complain that Sept- means seven then maybe shut up that bi- means two.'

Like most words for non-heterosexual identities and sexualities, 'bisexual' was forcibly applied to multi-gender attracted people as a way to pathologize and 'other' our desires. The word was originally a way to describe flowers with both male and female genitalia. Makes sense, right? Two sexes = bisexual. These types of flowers were also known as 'perfect' flowers, which is where the meme of putting (perfect) in brackets after the word bisexual comes from.

Our loveliness aside, the word 'bisexual' was used from 1824 onwards as a way of medicalizing people whom we would consider intersex today. From there, it was applied to people 'attracted to both sexes' in 1892, in the translation of Richard von Krafft-Ebing's *Psychopathia Sexualis*, which was one of the first books on sexual pathology. Sigmund Freud then discussed it in his book *Three Contributions to the Theory of Sex* (1920), arguing that all humans are born bisexual, and then grow into a developed sexuality of straight or gay. Yeah, our buddy Freud is responsible for the 'it's just a phase' stereotype. We'll come back to this later.

BI THE WAY

I suppose what being Bi and Non-Binary/Gender Fluid (still can't quite nail what I fit into!) is an expression of myself, and the answer to why I spent a large part of my life with this nagging feeling of not fitting in. I came out as Bi at 30 and that was enough to unpack without starting to look at how I felt gender-wise. I remember very distinctly my wife putting makeup on me before a Lady Gaga concert about 18 months ago, me looking in the mirror and a voice saying 'Oh, there you are.' My sexuality and gender don't really influence each other too much, in as much as the way I express myself physically has little to do with who I am attracted to. I'm attracted to men for a particular set of reasons, in the same way that I'm attracted to women or people who identify as neither for their own sets of reasons, how I'm feeling gender-wise doesn't necessarily interact with that. If I'm feeling particularly feminine one day it won't change my attraction to a woman, or vice versa. I suppose in queer spaces I'm more likely to be attracted to guys because it's more permitted! It makes me sad when people say bi is binary. I love being bisexual, and the LGBTQ+ community has given me an identity and a sense of belonging that I never dreamed possible. But I tire of the arguments over definitions and 'rules' regarding terminology.

James Luxford

What's in a name?

In the same way that 'homosexual' was popularized as a way of labelling same-sex desire as a mental illness or deficiency, so was bisexual. Unlike 'homosexuals', bisexuals never adopted a less medicalized moniker, like 'gay' or 'lesbian'. The term 'ambisexual' was proposed as a substitute in the early 20th century, but it didn't really catch on and 'bisexual' instead found its way into general use in the 1950s.

Whilst most people just use the shortening bi nowadays, I've come across many people for whom the label bi/bisexual makes them squirm because it has 'sex' in it. I used to feel this way too, which I discussed in an article I wrote for bi.org, entitled 'What It's Like to Be Out But Not Out-Out as a Bisexual' (Shearing 2017): 'I often find that thanks to some heavily internalized biphobia, telling people what kind of *sexual* I am feels just as scary as telling them I like girls. Worse than that sometimes, it feels dirty.'

So could finding a new word for 'bisexual' help avoid people thinking it's about the gender binary or sex? Some people certainly think so. Some people have suggested we retire 'bisexual' in favour of 'pan' or 'poly' (although because many Polynesian people have pointed out that as they already use that shortener to self-identify, it can be appropriative to use it as a stand in for polysexual or polyamorous) or any number of other words (my personal favourite suggestions is 'switchhitter', although this

can also have the connotation of switching between two things).
Even as I put out a call on Twitter for testimonials for this chapter, someone replied to tell me that most non-binary people
prefer pan, because it's 'more inclusive'. People who identify as bi
deal with this micro-aggression of telling us that our identifier
is outdated or doesn't mean what we say it means all the time.
This is most annoying for non-binary bisexual people who are
treated as if they are excluding themselves or assumed to be
uneducated on the existence of other terms and the supposedly
binary nature of bisexuality.

Beyond that, though, work to decouple 'bisexual' from meaning 'attracted to men and women' has been underway for as long
as bisexual activism itself. As we already explored in Chapter 1,
BiNet USA warned against assuming bi is binary in their 1990s
manifesto 'Anything that Moves':

> Do not assume that bisexuality is binary or duogamous in
> nature: that we have 'two' sides or that we must be involved
> simultaneously with both genders to be fulfilled human beings.
> In fact, don't assume that there are only two genders.

For myself and the other countless non-binary/genderfluid/
genderqueer/agender/bigender/etc. bisexual people, our existence itself should be proof enough that bisexuality and the bi
community isn't propping up the gender binary. No matter how
much people argue about semantics, the reality is that there are
bi people of every gender, and bi people having relationships
with people of every possible gender. Our lived experiences and
collective voice should have quashed this accusation decades
ago, and the fact it hasn't is evidence of the marginalization
and erasure of bi lives and voices; we are still fighting to be seen
as we are and to define ourselves. 'Knowing the long history of

attempts to obliterate bisexuality using the "reinforcing" trope, it is difficult for me to view this as anything other than part of the systematic erasure of bisexuality from queer communities,' writes bi and trans activist Julia Serano in her essay 'Bisexuality Does Not Reinforce the Gender Binary' (2018).

BI THE WAY

I couldn't properly comprehend my sexuality until I came at it from the perspective of being a man. I used to identify as closest to pan until very shortly after I came out as trans because I couldn't position myself in romantic or sexual relationships as a girl. Though I knew I wasn't asexual or aromantic because I did desire people, I felt like I didn't really have a sexuality at all so went for pan. All options were equally confusing and only appealing in an abstract theory. I was especially uncomfortable with lesbians or straight men being attracted to me – the latter of which was easier to rationalize, but the former made me feel like a bad and lesbophobic person so I ignored that in favour of 'working through my lesbophobia'. I couldn't be straight and I couldn't be gay, but I didn't feel like I could be bisexual. I think subconsciously because of the definition 'attraction to the same and different genders' was also a factor in me not feeling able to be bi, as was internalized biphobia. After I came out as trans, I made the mental switch to feeling right calling myself a bisexual, even though my experience of bisexuality is that bi groups and spaces are female dominated I felt more welcome and right there than I had ever done when I was identifying as a girl.

Tristan

I see a lot of overlap between the fight for trans equality and bi equality. Not necessarily in the minutiae – trans and non-binary people are still fighting for legal recognition of their gender and adequate healthcare (that's not to say bi people aren't fighting for the latter; we'll talk about that in the chapter on biphobia) – but in the ideology that oppresses us both.

Transphobia and biphobia are both a reaction to a challenge of the binaries our society relies on: both the gender binary and sexual binary. Those binaries allow one group to be elevated neatly above the other: men above women and heterosexuals above homosexuals. But when those binaries become blurry, when you can't tell what gender or sexuality someone is by looking at them or knowing their romantic/sexual partners, you can't maintain that hierarchy.

That's not to say that women and gay people haven't worked to undo that hierarchy (except maybe traditionalist women), but that in doing so many feminist and gay movements have thrown trans and bi people under the bus. We can see this most in focus in the rise of so-called left-wing transphobia in the UK. A small section of women, calling themselves 'gender-critical feminists', have launched a war of attrition against trans people, under the guise of protecting the rights of women and lesbians (many of us have tried pointing out that trans people can be both those things, but have had no joy). This farce has reached the point where straight media personalities like Graham Linehan and Sara Ditum can take aim at (cis) bi people in the name of protecting (cis) lesbians. When asked about bi/pan/queer people, Linehan implied on Twitter that the term 'queer' is used by people to appropriate gay struggles, while Ditum shared her thoughts on the same platform that bisexuality erases women in a leap of logic I'll never have the time or patience to untangle.

BI THE WAY

I'm a non-binary person and I identify as bisexual. I think most of the language we currently have for sexuality and gender falls short of my experience. I've had a lot of conversations with friends about non-binary vs genderqueer vs genderfluid vs enby etc. Some people don't like non-binary because it still defines in relationship to a binary. The truth is that non-binary is the best descriptor I have for how I move through the world. I don't like using words like genderqueer or genderfluid because I don't think that my gender is actually that fluid or changing, at least any more than anyone changes as they grow and age. As for sexuality: I find pretty much every word regarding sexuality falls short of what I want it to express. I feel like every word we have starts from a place of the person being talked about having a gender. Within the umbrella of non-binary I most closely identify with being agender. So since most of the words we have presume a gender, then where does this leave me? I like to say that my lack of gender makes me gay in every direction, or that it means that anyone who finds me attractive is now gay. Really, I'll use any word for sexuality to refer to myself.

I've got a 'this system is terrible so I'm destroying it and claiming it all for myself' kind of mentality. But at the same time, we still have to live in that system! So I identify as bisexual because I am attracted to people across the gender universe, and I think that there is a political power to the word 'bisexual'. There's so much stigmatization around bisexual people and I want to include myself in that number as a means of support and solidarity. As for how my gender and sexuality influence each other, I don't know if I have a coherent answer for that. I've dated both men and women, and my current partner is also non-binary. I was only ever out as non-binary while dating women. But before I was out, I did find myself changing my behaviours depending on the gender of the person I was dating, but I think that has less to do with my gender and more to do with patterns of behaviour I'd adopted to subconsciously handle being in the closet (I was convinced that being a woman was just a set of rules I had to learn and I just hadn't figured them out yet and so if I fit the perfect form of being a girlfriend, that would solve it). When I was out and dating women, I sometimes felt like I was being pressured into playing particular roles, like they wanted me to be a Butch, and while I have masculine traits and a very deep love and respect for Butches, I'm not a Butch. In my current relationship with a non-binary person I don't feel pressure to present or act in any particular gendered way. My partner and I are both bisexual but we also throw around words of gayness and homosexuality, particularly for each other. When people say that 'bi' is 'binary', it just makes me feel like they don't get it. All language for gender and sexuality is made up and should be fun. Putting these rules around it, and particularly putting rules restricting what other people are using for themselves, is the sort of pedantry that I feel like we should be trying to get rid of.

Anonymous

Libby Baxter-Williams, the director of Biscuit and an accomplished bi activist, often uses the phrase 'scratch a transphobe and you'll find a biphobe' to express how often these two prejudices overlap. And in my experience, this has held true. I've never met a transphobe who wasn't in some way biphobic, because both come from the same root.

Bisexuals vs essentialism

In many ways, feminism and gay rights movements have allowed biphobia and transphobia to grow among their ranks by attempting to fight the hierarchy, but not the binary it rests on. TERFs (trans-exclusionary radical feminists) argue that being a woman is about having a womb/vagina because they think that makes it easier to fight for spaces and rights for women. Some gay movements argue that they deserve equality because being gay is innate and something they can't change. In either scenario, someone 'deciding' to be a woman or date someone of the same gender when they have other options undermines the argument. Often, in leftist/queer/feminist circles, biphobia and transphobia are a reaction to this apparent betrayal of the cause.

So in my eyes (and in the eyes of many other writers and activists), part of fighting against transphobia and biphobia is fighting the notions of gender and sexual *essentialism*.

Essentialism is the concept that everything in a category must have something in common that makes them that thing: the essence of what they are. Essentialism is the 'belief that the everyday categories in the world around us have some deep underlying basis to them. If you look around the world and see different birds, you'll notice that they're all very different from one another, from ostriches to penguins to sparrows, and so forth. But if you're an essentialist, you think that there's some quality that they all have in common. Some may be hidden, non-obvious qualities that make them all birds—that make them what they are and gives them their identity and is responsible for why they all have certain ways of behaving and certain properties. It's an assumption that the world is not just how it looks on the surface but that there's another layer underneath that can explain the structure of the world,' explains Dr Susan Gelman in a 2012 interview with Annual Reviews.

Essentialism can be useful in scientific pursuits because it drives us to keep exploring the commonalities between things in a category to find out what they really are, but it is often damaging when applied to humans. For example, gender essentialism, the theory that genders have a physical essence, usually cited as reproductive organs or chromosomes, is weaponized against trans people to deny their gender.

Sexual essentialism, then, says that there is an essence – usually chromosomal – which unites all lesbians, gay men, straight people, bisexuals, etc. as the category that we are. This is of course mostly damaging because scientists continue to attempt to locate 'the gay gene', and it's easy to imagine what some people and governments would do with the ability to detect queerness at a biological level. In my opinion, it's also damaging as it is suggesting queerness is innate and limits our ability to explore the possibilities of sexual fluidity and self-determination.

Don't get me wrong; I'm not saying being queer is a choice. I'm saying, so what if it were? Why shouldn't we deserve to have our gender identities and sexualities respected even if we did choose them? To me, the 'born this way' narrative has left a lot of queer people out in the cold, and subtly suggests 'we would be like you [straight and cis] if we could'. However, I respect that this sentiment has done a *lot* of good for the LGBTQIA+ rights movement and that I enjoy a lot of rights and freedoms that I wouldn't if it hadn't been for that sentiment. I also understand that a lot of people do feel like they were born this way – hell, I do too – and that their sexuality is completely fixed, and I respect that totally. I just wish there were more room within queer circles to explore the possibility that some of us don't feel like we were born the way we now identify and that our sexuality may change and develop, even with our input, as we grow.

The approach that I and subsequently this book takes is a constructivist one: i.e. sexuality and gender are social constructs. This doesn't mean that our feelings about our own gender and the genders we desire aren't real, but that the circles we draw around them in order to categorize them only exist because our society does. One way to think of this is that in a parallel universe where humans exist but our history and understanding of religion, culture, science, language, and colonialism don't, the categories of man, woman, non-binary, gay, straight, bi, ace probably wouldn't exist. Liz A. Highleyman explains in her essay 'Identity and Ideas: Strategies for Bisexuals':

> The difference between essentialism and social constructionism is not one of 'nature versus nurture'. While it has probably always been the case that different people have had different attractions, constructionists believe that the meaning attached to those attractions is culturally specific. In a society in which the sexes were seen as equal, or in which a binary conception of sex and gender did not exist, people might not feel the need to classify themselves according to the sex/gender to which they are attracted (just as today someone may prefer people with blue eyes, yet not identify as a 'bluist' nor feel they are part of a 'blue-sexual community'). (Highleyman 1995, p.74)

I've seen essentialist ideas seep more and more into popular queer discourse over the last few years. Mostly from young queers and mostly in jest without explicitly referring to essentialism. I see it in the ever-growing meme trends such as 'all tops do X' or 'you're bottom if you do Y' about behaviours and traits that have nothing to do with sexual preferences. I see it too in the memes about lesbian/gay/bi/trans/ace etc. culture (we'll talk about this in depth in later chapters), which assign sometimes seemingly random preferences and personalities to all people of a certain identity. Again, I understand that these are mostly just jokes and attempts from young, often isolated people to feel part of a community. But I also am seeing, mostly online, a trend of mass harassing or dogpiling people who denounce or reject essentialist approaches to sexuality/gender and aligning this rejection of essentialism with invalidation of queer identities. 'To prescribe a range of interests, behaviors and values is a form of essentialism – sometimes predicated on exactly the loaded stereotypes that we have so long sought to avoid,' writes Michael Amherst in his book exploring bisexuality, *Go the Way Your Blood Beats* (2018, p.99).

I, and many others, have pointed out the connection between the trend of young queers strictly policing their own and each other's identities – down to fixed labels, and completely separate yet concurrent histories, cultures, and reclaimed slurs of LGBTQIA+ identities – and the resurgence of exclusionary, lesbian separatist, essentialist politics. Heather Hogan, the manager of queer women's digital magazine *Autostraddle*, wrote about this phenomenon on Tumblr in 2017:

These [online lesbian-separatist] spaces that use the word 'lesbophobia' to attack trans and bi women or people who use the word queer share more than than [*sic*] an ideology with Breitbart. You'll find them saying things like 'trans women want to colonize the lesbian community'. You'll find them using the phrase 'SJW' (meaning Social Justice Warrior), a pejorative term coined by the Men's Rights Activist movement. And you'll find a lot of talk about how the correct 'biology' is the thing that allows people access to the protections of the majority. And lots and lots and lots and lots of just truly sickening propaganda leveled at trans and bi women. It's very much about creating an in-group and scapegoating an out.

To be clear, I am not placing the responsibility for trans/biphobia at the feet of lesbians, or even lesbian separatists. These prejudices exist because of the structure of cisnormativity and monosexism upheld by cisgender, heterosexual people in order to retain their unearned privileges. This is a big topic, so we'll build on it more in the chapters about community and biphobia.

What about bisexuality and gender expression?

So, if bi people are and date people of any gender, how does the bi community express our genders? If the mainstream media is to be believed, bisexuality only exists in the form young, white, super-feminine cisgender women. But that couldn't be further from the truth! Bisexual people have always come in all shapes, sizes, genders, and gender expressions.

Hold up though; what's the difference between gender identity and gender expression? While gender expression is linked to gender identity and sex, the two aren't always aligned or reliant on each other. Morgan Lev Edward Holleb describes the difference in *The A-Z of Gender and Sexuality*:

The gender(s) that someone is expressing with their outward appearance, including their body language, vocal mannerisms, make up, accessories, clothes and the way they relate to other people. (p.132)

67

I highly recommend reading the rest of Morgan's explanation of gender identity, as it has a very useful exploration of how gendered cues are connected to displays of weakness (femininity) and strength (masculine), which we don't have much space to cover here.

So, if gender is part of who someone *is*, gender expression is how they *tell* you. It can also be a way of sending a message about how to treat someone in regard to their gender, or it can even be a political statement. For example, butch/masculine women still identify/are recognizable as women but they use their gender expression to send a message about how they perceive what it means to be a women.

Gender expression can also be used to send a message about sexuality, and it is often used as a way to stereotype people as to how they might sexually identify. Masculine women are assumed to be lesbians, and feminine men are assumed to be gay. On the flip side, feminine women and masculine men are nearly always read as straight. You might have noticed these stereotypes ignore bisexuality altogether and take a binary approach to both sexuality and gender, once again ignoring the existence of anyone outside of our binarist approach to the world.

These stereotypes have negative effects for pretty much everyone. In her essay 'Too Butch to Be Bi', Robin Sweeney discusses the isolation of being a butch bi women. In both bi and butch communities, she felt like an outsider for either her butchness or her bi-ness and struggled with the constant erasure of her bisexuality. She also discusses how many butch women assume they must be lesbians and feel like failures or traitors to butch lesbian communities when they find themselves attracted to men. Unfortunately, this feeling is often made worse as many lesbians believe bi women shouldn't call themselves butch/femme, because they are words that only apply to people who aren't attracted to men (we'll get into why so many bi people and lesbians disagree with this in a minute). Robin writes:

> [But] once we find a community that is accepting of our same-sex interests, we run into an entirely different series of messages. A number of these are about appearances and what they are supposed to say about who we are. The ideas about femmes (femme women aren't really interested in other women, femme men aren't really interested in women at all) and butches (butches are always the aggressors in sex, whether they are men or women) permeate our queer culture. These ideas make it difficult for us to explore who we are and who we want to be. Many people feel too threatened to challenge the status quo of an already fringe community, for fear of being outcast from the one place where they have struggled to belong. (p.185)

Robin's essay was published in the '80s, but four decades later lots of butch and gender non-conforming women still feel the same way. 'It's often assumed I'm gay or in a phase of accepting I'm gay rather than simply happy being quite open to who I'm attracted to. It's made me doubt myself thinking maybe they are right and I am just in denial about being gay. Or maybe I'm not "gay" enough to be part of this community,' explains Beth Ingham, a butch bi woman who reached out to chat to me about this topic. 'Yet I've also grown up constantly being told I'm not "girly" or embracing my femininity enough. Or that maybe I'm focusing more on women because I'm worried men wouldn't like me for me and my style. I get the homophobic response from society because of how I present and who I'm attracted to/the community I spend my time in but also the biphobia if I mention that I'm not always just attracted to women, both inside the community and in wider society.

Sometimes it's just easier to let people assume I'm a lesbian as it makes me feel more accepted and like there's a clear path for me in the LGBTQI community, but maybe some people would say that's problematic and I contribute to my own erasure,' she continues.

BI THE WAY

In a sense, my gender expression is my way of asserting my queerness as well as a defence mechanism against fetishization by straight men. I do stand-up comedy and often dress butch to perform it, partly because I feel more comfortable on stage in it, partly because talking about looking like a boy while being bisexual is now a firm part of my comedy routine. I think there is also a part of me that feels like I will not be taken seriously by audiences as a queer person, and might get fetishized, if I dressed femme.

Currently, I am dating a cishet man who likes women who look butch. I have not come out to him as non-binary yet. This is my first serious relationship with a cishet white guy and I often feel the need to dress butch to assert my queerness, though more and more often I find I don't really care if I don't think about it.

There is a misogynist and classist stigma [in the UK] about Asian women who go with white men. They are assumed to be vapid, shallow, unintelligent, hyperfemi-nine, hypersexual, materialistic, submissive, among other things. Both of us sort of enjoy breaking that stereotype because of how I look. Once again, looking GNC (gender non-conforming) is a sort of defence mechanism.

Stephani Dogfoot

As someone who falls on the 'masc-of-centre' side of things, I often feel the same. When I was younger, I internalized the stereotype that by being or identifying as 'butch' or 'butchy femme' and dating men I was responsible for the way men who don't take butch lesbian's identities seriously continue to pursue or fetishize them. But now I understand that queer women are not responsible for the way straight men fetishize us. If all bi women stopped identifying as butch (or femme), straight men would not suddenly take lesbians' rejection or identities more seriously. To claim bi women make men think queer women are available to them is biphobic and subtly shifts the blame back onto bi women when we are assaulted/harassed by men by suggesting we are inherently available to them and lead them on.

For Kitty Cullen, the combination of heteronormativity, gender expectations, and anti-blackness have had a big impact on her coming out and her gender presentation. 'I've faced criticism, and disapproval for instances where I wasn't conforming to the traditional femme standards, for dressing in ways that prized comfort over the expectations, and perceptions of others (some of this was rooted in classism). This was/is especially the case when I am engaging with my home culture, where everyone knows everyone, and deviation can come with all sorts of implications, and loss of social capital. There's also the fact that many of the cisheteronormative standards for my gender role are interwoven with anti-Blackness – how I am allowed to style my hair, what ways are safest for me to present without losing the protection of my humanity, the expectations of what is/is not normal for my body, pressures to heighten or aspire to white Euro-associated features in order to attract cishet men, etc., and of course facing overall censure from cishet relatives to fit "appropriate" moulds that were passed down during the colonisation of my country. Under these pressures, I developed self-consciousness about my body, discomfort with experimenting with my style, trying things that might have brought more attention to myself, or doing anything that would have made me less attractive to cishet men,' she explains to me in a conversation over email.

She also finds the argument that bi/pan (Kitty identifies as demi-pan grey-ace) people can't use the terms butch or femme to be particularly frustrating. 'I think it's ridiculous that we've arrived at a point where monoromantic/sexual lesbians have gained exclusive ownership of terms that were never only theirs. To force bi+ people out of labels that were initially ours, then re-define who is included in them, is insulting. It is especially egregious given the contributions of bi+ people to the sapphic (women attracted to women) community. We've always been here. The terms have always been ours. And you cannot steal our labour, and terms from us, then be offended when people refuse to abandon them, or choose to reclaim them if they so identify. In short, I think some people should make themselves familiar with whatever queer history is available to us all, before making claims to exclusive ownership of anything.'

She continues: 'The point of queerness is not to reproduce the systems, and ideas that harm us; it is to dismantle them, and make space for a spectrum of experiences. That means recognising that gender expression is not an indicator of romantic, or sexual orientation. Making assumptions about what women desire, or do not desire based on their dress reinforces stereotypes, and inaccurate ideas about women of all orientations. It forces those who aren't queer into boxes, and labels they did not ascribe to themselves, and makes actual queer women feel like they are existing incorrectly in their queerness, or do not belong to their communities. Also, we really need to consider what it means to cling to practices born out of trauma, and necessity (signalling queerness through dress, and accessories) without (re-)examination of their purposes, and meaning; or recognition that these practices must evolve with our own efforts to exist outside of traditional structures. It is not enough to expand definitions to include your own nonconformity, presentation, or attractions, only to create new constraints, and places for marginalisation, or exclusion. We must do *more*. That means breaking down our own expectations, and examining them for what they are; then, creating something that encompasses the gender expression, identity, and sexual/romantic orientation of all people.'

In the last few years, some butch/gender non-conforming celebrities such as Kristen Stewart have fought back against the 'hypersexual, feminine, bi girl' fantasy that is often the only way the media ever acknowledges bisexuality/pansexuality (and often lesbians, too).

Personally, I've always been a tomboy, and playing with different aspects of gender is an important part of who I am. I get bored easily in general and changing up my look and messing with people's expectations is one of the most liberating and exciting things about being queer. As a teenager, I wore too much eyeliner and red lipstick that I stole my from mum, but I also had cropped black hair and wore boy's patent leather shoes to school. I was one of only a few openly bi people most of my friends and school peers knew, and I think to them it made sense that I presented as both 'sort-of-a-boy' and 'sort-of-a-girl' if I liked both (and more). I think this assumption still persists for gender non-conforming bi people. In the same way gay people used to be considered 'inverts' – as in containing the 'opposite' gender in order to be attracted to the same gender – some people may still assume that bi people contain 'both genders' in order to be attracted to 'both' genders. As bisexual activist and author of Bi: *Notes for a Bisexual Revolution* (2013a), Shiri Eisner explains:

Bisexuality creates 'gender trouble', which places bisexual people outside the culturally legitimate boundaries of male and female. In addition, bisexuals have often been imagined as being psychologically 'both male and female' since their 'male side desires women' and 'their female side desires men'. (p.244)

My gender identity and expression have always been closely linked to my bisexuality. Like a lot of bi genderfluid/genderqueer people, I can be a bit of gender-chameleon; I often notice my gender identity and expression shifting to mimic the people I have crushes on. As my tastes encompass pretty much all of the gender universe, so does my own identity/expression. Now that I'm out and comfortable in my sexuality and gender identity, I've started to be a lot more playful with how I express them both. I like flagging my bisexuality with a side-shave and short hair paired with a deep love of makeup. My go-to aesthetic is a full face of makeup with hair done and jewellery, paired with an androgynous baggy T-shirt, jeans, and Doc Martens. Mixing and matching different aspects of femininity, androgyny, and masculinity is part of what feels so freeing about my bi identity; I can be as fluid and 'in-between' as I want.

BI THE WAY

Being femme for me has to do with being feminine, but also rejecting traditional femininity and womanhood. I'm not feminine for men, as society at large would like to assume. I am for myself, and to a lesser but still strong extent, other women. The way I present myself and act with my attraction to men is entirely separate from my femme identity. It ties into my non-binary identity as well because while I don't mind being referred to as a woman,

> femme for me encompasses the idea that while I am fem-
> inine, I'm not necessarily completely a woman. It's a good
> way for me to be like 'yes I am feminine, woman aligned,
> and attracted to other woman aligned people, but I'm not
> ENTIRELY just a woman' if that makes sense.
>
> Kelli

For queer femmes, assumptions that they must be straight are equally damaging. In an article reacting to being told she couldn't call herself femme, Janis Luna (2018) writes '*I am queer,*...and...it took me a long time to get to this place of authenticity about it, specifically because of the way femme-invisibility, and the erasure of bisexual identities, compound each other' (emphasis in original). The combination of both femininity and bisexuality being assumed as being performed/for men means that many femme bisexual women deeply struggle to be their authentic self and to explore their attraction to multiple genders. After reading around about femme bisexuality and asking several femme bis themselves, I came across a very common concern: 'Am I actually performing femininity for myself, or because I can't shake off the need for men's approval?' You may have noticed that this is a lot like another doubt most bisexual women have internalized: 'Am I really attracted to men, or am I just unable to move past compulsory heterosexuality?' Dominique, a femme bisexual woman, reached out to me on Twitter to explain why she struggles with her femme bi identity sometimes:

On a superficial level, [being a bi femme] means sharing make-up with my femme partners and sharing belts with my masc partners. It also means an equal opportunity strap. But in truth, there's sometimes a feeling that I'm 'passing' in a way that feels uncomfortable and erases my identity. A continuous question of am I performing gender for my authentic self or comfort in society? My femme characteristics do conflict with roles that are unfortunately set by patriarchal standards that are internalized in my relationships, so I do a constant evaluation of myself and my interactions with my community and the larger world.

BI THE WAY

I've typically presented as femme for the past 20 years but do not act or perceive myself as femme. My relationships with women have mostly been with femmes, but I've been married to a bi man for 13 years. I also feel presenting as femme was even more of an invitation to biphobia when I was first coming out, getting called out by drag queens because of my long hair and large breasts (the latter I inherited). I suffered a lot of gatekeeping from [young queer women] and queer men back then, who would corner me at bars and demand to know what I was doing there or if I was 'really a lesbian' or a 'tourist'. To be honest, I still can't say at 45 how much of my femme presentation is learned behaviour to fit into my family and broader society and how much is innate to me. I fix things, talk, and often interact like a man, lack maternal characteristics, hate shopping and other femme-stereo-typical activities. I've often joked I just don't female well. Ultimately, I'm probably by today's definitions genderqueer or enby, or maybe just a butch who loves lipstick and calling people pet names. All that to say, because gender and presentation are so complex, I try not to make so many assumptions about other people based only on where they might be outwardly perceived to fall on the masc–femme scale, despite constantly facing the assumptions made about me.

Anita Dolman

What about bi men?

In general there's a lot less discourse around bi men and gender within the LGBTQIA+ community, for several reasons. First, because there are much fewer bi men out and vocal about their sexuality, but possibly also because male privilege means that even (cis) queer men have a lot less to argue about when it comes to how queerness, gender expression, and relations to/with men affects their position in society, compared to women.

Bisexual activist Vaneet Mehta gave me some insight into what it's like to be a femme bi man: 'I've always been labelled as gay (or more accurately, a "batty boy" when I was growing up). Even after coming out, being slightly femme-of-center meant that the assumption is that I'm gay. This comes from all sides. Family, friends, randoms on the internet,' he explained.

If gender expression is just another way in which bisexuality is erased from popular discourse and used to undermine bi experiences, let's get into exploring how bi people come out, fight erasure, and live as our proud selves.

CHAPTER 4

When Should I Come Out?

first came out when I was 14, at an Alice Cooper concert in Brighton.

My best friend and I had seats in the balcony and were watching as the standing attendants filtered into the pit. We pointed out attractive men to each other, slightly drunk off our newfound interest in men and relationships and the power our bodies could have. Honestly, we were the youngest attendants by at least ten years, and looking back I'm sure they were all gross. But whether they were actually attractive wasn't the point of the game.

I pointed out a woman dressed as the nurse of death. 'She's hot.' My friend didn't reply. We pointed out a few more men. I pointed out another nurse. A few more men. Another nurse. A few more men. Another nur—

'Do you like girls too?' she asked. I nodded, or stuttered something – I don't really remember – but my stomach turned itself inside out. I held my breath.

'Cool,' she said. And there it was. I was bisexual and Alice Cooper came on stage dressed in a disco-ball suit and opened with 'School's Out'.

Several years later, that same friend came out to me as bi as well. She told me just as I was pulling onto a roundabout and I almost crashed my car in excitement.

There's no right or wrong time to come out. I started my coming-out journey in my early teens; my friend started hers at the beginning of her 20s. Some people don't come out until they're middle-aged or older. Some people never come out. The decision is always deeply personal, and you shouldn't let others influence your decision.

The point of this chapter is not to tell you when to come out, or even to make you feel like you have to. Its aim is to help you understand what it means to come out and be out as a bi person. To do this, we'll explore personal stories, statistics, and biphobia to hopefully equip you with the tools to decide when or if to start your coming-out journey.

BI THE WAY

I personally have never identified as straight or gay and, despite having grown up with no LGBTQ community/influence, I was kinda stubborn and forward-thinking about the whole coming out thing. I didn't feel a need to tell anyone because 'straight people don't come out, why should I?' and I figured that if I ever got a girlfriend then I'd just tell my mum that I had a girlfriend. However, my sister beat me to it:

My sister [to my mum when I was about 18? in an attempt to get me into trouble]: You know they're bi, don't you?

My mum: Yeah, and?

I am out to everyone now, but bisexual culture is having to out yourself over and over for all of eternity.

> There's always new people and assumptions made. People forget or decide on your sexuality based on who you're currently seeing or having sex with. I've even had people within the queer community tell a female partner that I'm gay, despite the fact they've seen me regularly attend a play party that was for women and trans people...
>
> *Liam*

Since that December night in Brighton, I've come out thousands of times. Some have been big, like coming out to my parents, but most have been little corrections when people have made assumptions about my sexuality. Despite what we may see in the (very limited) films and TV shows about being queer, coming out is not a single, grand gesture. Because of the heteronormative culture we live in, everyone is assumed straight until proven queer. That means that even if we've come out to some people in our lives, everyone else will most likely still assume we're straight and cis. Things are more complicated for non-monosexual people who may be in relationships that others perceive as being 'straight'. As we've already explored in the last chapter, people tend to make binarist assumptions about others' sexuality based on the (perceived) gender of their current partner. This can make it very tricky for bi people in monogamous relationships to come out.

Bi erasure

To help explain this, 'bi erasure' is the term popularized by bi activists for the process of bi lives, experiences, and issues being ignored or purposely excluded from discussions and resources that affect or are relevant to us, including denying the existence of bi identities outright. Bi erasure is so prevalent that lots (I would dare to say most) bi people have had to come out again and again to the same people, because of the assumption that the bi person is now straight/gay depending on the most recent person we were dating or intimate with. This is an almost universal micro-aggression that bi people face, and it's a common theme among memes and jokes shared by bi communities. (See Chapter 8 for more on bi erasure.)

But while we find humour in people's 'forgetfulness', having to constantly remind and reaffirm our identity to people is frustrating and invalidating, and takes a toll on our collective mental health. It takes a lot to build up the courage to come out to people; to then have them deny, erase, or even forget who you are based on their assumptions about your relationships is hurtful. Many bi people, especially those in long-term relationships, can't find the courage or energy to continually come out. Back in 2017, I wrote about this feeling in my article 'What It's Like to Be Out But Not Out-Out as a Bisexual':

It may seem trivial, but after working for years to come out to yourself and accept your sexuality, having people dismiss it and refuse to listen feels belittling and frustrating, especially when coming from gay people who experience the same dismissal from straight people that we do. (Shearing 2017)

In Bi: Notes for a Bisexual Revolution, Shiri offers up an alternative term for this experience: 'coercive passing'. Shiri explains:

Whereas invisibility suggests that one is simply 'unseen' in their marginalized identity, the concept of coercive passing suggests that one isn't simply invisible but actively perceived

81

as something other than they experience themselves to be (as influenced by social construction and power hierarchies). Thus, being 'invisible' in fact means being actively, coercively passed off as a member of the default/hegemonic group, entailing erasure as well as more subtle forms of oppression. This is particularly relevant to the concept of bisexual invisibility – taken from this perspective, it's easy to understand that bisexuality and bisexual people are not invisible, but are being actively and coercively erased. (Eisner 2013a, p.107)

I like this explanation because it takes into account how often bi people are trying to be out and visible but are actively passed as monosexual, particularly if they are dating/married to someone of a different gender and therefore assumed to be straight. If you google 'I'm married, but I'm still bi', you'll be returned 73,000,000 results. While this isn't exactly a scientific study, for me it suggests the sheer volume of people struggling to be seen as their true selves while being coercively passed because of their relationship.

BI THE WAY

The actual coming out was fairly painless in the end; it was the build up to it and the wrestling with self-erasure that was the painful bit – I came out late (just this year!), and only really came out to myself last year. And because I'm married, the bit I struggled with was on the one hand the need to be honest (I was drowning in depression because of the usual effects of the closet, and the defence barriers built up over the years meant I was shutting down emotionally) but then the fear that even if my wife could accept me as I am, this was bound to put unfounded worries in her own mind thanks to other people's misconceptions. So it felt like a selfish act – trading my sanity for hers. And I told myself why did it matter anyway – I'm happily married. For all intents and purposes, I'm straight. Self-erasure!

James

The impact of bi erasure

As well as re-closeting and coercively passing people who are trying to come out, bi erasure can have a big impact on people realizing their sexuality to begin with. As you might notice throughout this chapter, lots of people's coming out stories include feelings of 'If I'm attracted to [someone of the same gender] I must be gay' or 'I can't be queer if I still like different-gendered people' because there's such a lack of representation of bisexuality and multi-gender attraction within mainstream culture. In fact, I don't think I read a single story or talked to a single person for this chapter who didn't express a similar sentiment.

GLAAD's 'Where We Are on TV' report (2012) regularly shows that bisexual characters/storylines grace our screens less frequently than gay/lesbian characters/storylines, although this is on the rise. Back in 2012, for example, GLAAD reported that there were 30 gay male characters on broadcast TV, 10 lesbians, 7 bi women, and 2 bi men. The report also shows that 78 per cent of LGBTQIA+ characters were white, 12 per cent were black, 5 per cent were Asian Pacific Islander characters, 4 per cent were Latinx, and 1 per cent were other. It also reported only one trans character and seemingly two LGBTQIA+ characters with disability. The report does not break down the sexual orientation of these characters, but we know at least one was bi: Callie Torres in *Grey's Anatomy*, played by the incredible Sara Ramirez. This lack of representation would have had a huge impact on disabled, non-white, and trans bi people, who may never have seen themselves reflected in the public sphere. Not seeing ourselves and our experiences depicted makes it difficult both to recognize and articulate them. It can also lead to feelings of isolation, making it even harder to come out and seek community.

In 2019, the number reported by GLAAD jumped to 46 gay characters, 40 lesbians, 21 bi women, 9 bi men, and 2 bi non-binary characters. This increase not only reflects the increased visibility of LGBTQIA+ people in our culture but is also partly driven by the rise of streaming services such as Netflix, which tend to have more diverse stories and characters than broadcast television. There have also been big improvements in the representation for LGBTQIA+ people of colour, disabled, and trans queer people. 'For the first time, LGBTQ characters of color outnumber white LGBTQ characters on broadcast television, 50 percent to 49 percent. 44 percent of all series regulars on broadcast scripted television are people of color,' says the report (p.4). Whilst the amount of disabled queer characters had increased to 2.1 per cent, this is still not reflective of reality. The report also found that there were 26 trans characters on TV the previous year: 17 trans women, 5 trans men, and 4 non-binary characters. Two of those characters were bi. Whilst this is a notable improvement on previous years, there is still a long, long way to go when it comes to representing trans people and the gender diversity of the bi community.

Despite the much-improved numbers of bi characters on our screens, GLAAD notes that there is still a long way to go in terms of *positive* representation. From the GLAAD 2019–2020 'Where We Are on TV' report:

Previous editions of this report have noted several harmful tropes we still see being played out in regards to the treatment of bisexual+ characters. Some of these include:

- Treating a character's attraction to more than one gender as a temporary plot device;
- Depicting bisexual+ characters as inherently untrustworthy, scheming, obsessive, or as having self-destructive behaviors;
- Bi erasure, including bi characters who are never explicitly labeled as bisexual. While some people do prefer to not use a label, the outsized number of bi+ characters who never use a specific word for themselves (be it bi, pan, queer, fluid, or another) is a long-recurring problem. (GLAAD 2020)

As well as bi erasure in the media, lack of information about non-binary sexuality such as bisexuality in education, mainstream culture, and even within LGBTQIA+ communities has slowed down many people's coming-out journey. Despite this, studies show that bi people make up the majority of the rainbow community, so we're obviously a resilient bunch.

BI THE WAY

I never really had a moment of coming out, per se. I was asexual but didn't realize it until I was in my 20s, by which point I'd started to shift and be more bi – I discussed this with friends who were also in various stages of queer fluctuating identities, so it was never an announcement to anyone who didn't know. Because I didn't seriously

> date anyone in my 20s, it never seemed pertinent to tell my family. Then last year I sent a picture of me and E to my dad saying 'I'm dating someone!' And he replied, 'great, what's her name?' I never got to tell my mom, and I have no idea how she would have reacted – obviously not negatively, but I feel more concerned about 'what I'm doing with my life'.
>
> Stacy

Bi erasure and coercive passing are just some of the reasons why bi people have much lower rates of coming out compared to lesbian and gay people. Only 36 per cent of bi people are out to all their friends, compared to 74 per cent of lesbians/gay men, and only 20 per cent of bi people are out to all their family, compared to 63 per cent of lesbians/gay men according to Stonewall UK (Melville, Stonborough, and Gooch 2020). This number plunges to 12 per cent of bi men (there are not yet any statistics that take people of other genders into account). As I was searching these statistics, I noticed that an article has been published almost every year since 2011 all reporting the same trend from different reports. It infuriates me, then, that none of the major LGBTQIA+ organizations have ever done much to address why this is or what can be done about it. So, let's dive into it ourselves.

There are many factors that contribute to these numbers. One of the main reasons is the one that's going to be the hardest to overcome: for many bi people there are no benefits to coming out. Back in 2013, ScienceDaily published a story called 'It May Not "Get Better" for Bisexual Teens'. It explored how, while the It Gets Better Project, launched in 2010, had had an important impact on the lives of gay and lesbian teens, the same could not be said for bisexual teens. The It Gets Better Project, which was started in part by Dan Savage, was a social media campaign encouraging people to share their uplifting and empowering stories of coming out, in order to help young closeted people feel less alone. The study that ScienceDaily reported on, which was conducted by the Department of Educational, School, and Counseling Psychology at the University of Kentucky, sought to discover whether the high rates of depression and suicidal thoughts suffered by queer teens decreased at all as they aged. It is common knowledge that queer teens experience higher rates of mental illness than our straight counterparts, but it had not yet been explored as to whether these were alleviated as queer teens aged. To quote the findings from ScienceDaily (2013):

> Teens were divided into groups based on their self-reported identification as heterosexual, mostly heterosexual, gay, mostly gay or bisexual. The study found that depression symptoms, namely thoughts of suicide, decreased from 42 percent to 12.3 percent as teens in all groups transitioned into adulthood and suicide attempts decreased from 15.9 to 2.9 percent. But the 'mostly gay' and bisexual teens did not report a significant decrease in some measures of suicidal thoughts or behaviors.

After struggling to come out to themselves and loved ones, they weren't welcomed into a community of new queer friends and coming out didn't alleviate the many mental health issues associated with being closeted (perhaps because so many were coercively passed or re-closeted). 'Some bisexuals may struggle with depression later on because they don't feel accepted and supported in either lesbian and gay or straight communities. Bisexual identity does not fit into the gay/straight categories most people are comfortable with,' lead researcher Robert Cardom told ScienceDaily.

That the It Gets Better Project was overlooking bisexual teens was not much of a surprise to many bisexual activists, as Dan Savage had already made a name for himself as a biphobe. In 2011, he published a wildly biphobic article that hit basically every stereotype about bi people it possibly could and, a year later, he produced a series called *When We Rise*. In the eight hours of airtime about LGBTQIA+ history from the '70s to 2010, Savage did not include or mention a single bi activist or organization. As you'll see in the next chapter, this couldn't have been just an oversight; bi people have been embedded in the queer liberation movement since the beginning. And that leads us to the next factor that makes coming out difficult for bi people: lack of representation.

Lack of bi role models

BI THE WAY

I definitely think the complete lack of Bi role models and Bi representation in media negatively impacted my coming out. There were, in hindsight, opportunities to give us Bi representation but it was never done. The most notable one, for me, was Willow in *Buffy*. The first time she ever kissed Tara, her response was 'hello, gay now'. This was despite the fact that Willow had previously had a long-term boyfriend and had had multiple crushes on men. It sounded like a flip of a switch. And so, my inner monologue was built around this. Binary. You're straight or you're gay. That's that. Of course changing from straight to gay is also entirely valid, but the common use of that trope means Bi is never given a look in. If it did, I may have learnt about bisexual way earlier than I did. After discovering Bi, I became more aware of it. And with that, instances of Bi erasure. I remember an episode of *Glee* where Blaine thought he might be bi rather than gay, but eventually worked out that it was just the alcohol talking. I remember an episode of *90210* where Teddy slept with a man. He had been in relationships with women previously. My friend and housemate who also watched the show immediately said he was gay. When I pointed out that he could be Bi or questioning, she said no because he slept with a man. I wasn't out at this point. And this interaction definitely made me never want to come out. The lack of role models meant I felt alone and invalidated. I never saw Bi as an option because the world never presented it as one. Even real-life Bi people like Freddie Mercury were erased, being labelled as gay. If I saw Bi, just once, I may have come out sooner. For sure it would have at least been easier.

Vaneet Mehta

The lack of bi public figures or role models is another oft-cited reason for bi people's low coming-out rates. This is especially true for bi men and non-binary people. 'In the 2016 Workplace Equality Index, just 11 per cent of respondents felt there were enough bisexual role models in their workplace, compared to 53 per cent for gay role models, 42 per cent for lesbian role models and 19 per cent for trans* role models,' says the Mind pamphlet on bisexuality 'Stand Bi Me' (Mind 2017, p.5). As you can imagine, this can become something of a self-fulfilling prophecy: fewer bi people come out because they have fewer role models leading the way, meaning there are then fewer out bi people to be role models for those trying to come out, and the cycle continues. Role models can be an important aspect in helping people come out because they empower people to see that there's a path for those like them to be out and successful, as well as signalling that it's a safe place for people to bring their whole selves to work.

Women are also affected by this lack of role models and are less likely to be out in the workplace. A study conducted in Australia in 2018 by PwC found that bi women were half as likely to be out at work, compared to women who only described themselves as 'same sex attracted': 38 per cent compared with 78 per cent, respectively (Marks et al. 2018, p.11). One participant told the study: 'I'm bisexual but dating a man so feel it doesn't count' (Marks et al. 2018, p.5). Others described facing stereotypes in the workplace, including being considered 'attention-seeking, confused, promiscuous and greedy'. An article published by SBS, an Australian broadcaster, explains: 'Also, a fear of being judged and lack of understanding were risks identified as being more important for bi women in being out at work' (Melani 2019).

As well as a lack of role models, not feeling supported in the workplace is another reason bi people are less likely to be out at work. Many bi people feel that employee LGBT networks are not welcoming of bi people. These networks are perceived to be catering more to gay men and lesbians, with little focus or attention given to bi participants or issues, according to a study conducted by Stonewall (Chamberlain 2012, p.14). 'Most workplace LGBT networks are primarily lesbian and gay networks,' Marcus Morgan told the *Guardian* in 2012, 'Bisexual people have reported being made to feel unwelcome if they bring opposite sex partners to supposedly inclusive events' (Burston 2012).

BI THE WAY

So I grew up in what is essentially a Jewish Jehovah's Witnesses, so an ultra-orthodox, cult. I was always labelled a 'tomboy'. One day I turned to my mum and said I wanted to be a boy at about eight. I was beaten until I said I was lying and happy being a girl. It was decided I was too much of an evil influence and I was sent away to school so I didn't corrupt my sister.

I got a girlfriend at school who gave me a love bite, young love is so sweet, came home for the holidays and my parents saw and commented that at least I had a boyfriend. I corrected them (I wasn't that bright) it was just ignored.

I came out as a lesbian at 16 I just couldn't be inauthentic anymore (again not very bright) and I was called all sorts of things I was beyond help in their eyes so I was kicked out and on the streets.

I was desperate and made a desperate decision and joined a problematic organization. Built a group of lesbian friends was settled I was just a boyish lesbian. Then Sven happened. He was the most beautiful man that ever walked the planet (at the time) we got together, he saw something in me that I was unable to see in myself. Sadly he was killed. But he'd given me the strength to come out as Bi. Most of my lesbian friends were not cool with this and broke away.

Long time passes and I'm relatively happy being a Bi boyish woman. But I started hanging more with gender variant people and realized there was a name for the feelings inside me. So I tentatively came out as non-binary and in the last few months as a trans man. It's very early days and I still feel awkward when saying my pronouns or my transness as I feel like a fraud or like I just look like a massive girl.

Ymir

Coming out as bi

So what are the benefits of coming out? Despite research showing there are fewer benefits to coming out for bi+ people, there are still lots of reasons why people do it. For starters, the stress of hiding who you are or misleading people can have a negative impact on people's self-image and mental health. 'Hiding who you are can be a big struggle. It can take your focus and energy away from other important things in your life such as your job, studying for exams,' writes Stonewall UK on their website. For others – myself included, to some degree – coming out is a political statement; being open about who we are is about being visible for other non-straight people and speaking up for our community. Coming out in some situations can also be a way of (attempting) to access services that fully cater to who you are – like healthcare services, therapy, or communities. As the Bisexual Resource Center explains:

> Like lesbians, gay men and transgender people, bisexuals must weigh whether to come out to healthcare professionals. On one hand, we may fear a negative response and poor treatment; on

the other, our silence leaves providers with incomplete information and may put our mental and physical health at risk. (Bisexual Resource Center n.d.-b)

Despite biphobia in the LGBTQIA+ community, coming out and finding community has a very positive impact on a lot of people's lives. It can give us the opportunity to be around people like us, to feel less alone, to talk about our problems with people who understand, to find friends, or even to fall in love. A lot of bi activism has been about carving out spaces for bi people in a binary world, and there are lots of places – even if they are just online – where you can find support from other bi people. We have a whole chapter about it coming up soon (see Chapter 10).

For bisexual parents, coming out can also be a way of introducing their children to the non-binary nature of sexuality (and the world!) and helping to open their minds to the different ways in which families are formed, lives are lived, and loves are loved. But as we've already explored, coming out can be particularly difficult when you're in a long-term relationship or have children, as people around us make assumptions about our identity based on the gender of our current or most recent partner. This extends not only to people who see having children with someone as the ultimate way of proving your attraction to the gender of their co-parent (most likely someone of a different gender), but to children themselves.

'I always had been kind of open about my bisexuality around my daughter, keeping it age appropriate of course. Basically I never wanted her to feel uncomfortable about letting us know if she started questioning her own sexuality or gender identity,' explains bi parent Sharon Shaw. 'The actual "coming out" followed on from us talking about early crushes on animated characters, and I mentioned a male and a female one. She checked to make sure she'd understood me right and then we carried on with the conversation. No weirdness or drama. I don't think it changed her perspective at all; she's always been very supportive of LGBTQ concepts, Pride etc., and seems to consider herself bi too, although she's only 11 so I expect some degree of fluidity!'

For bi+ activist Heron Greenesmith, the decision to come out to their child was very straightforward. 'I am committed to being open to the kid about myself as a person. And to be a model in the ways I can. So she knows about my anxiety and depression, my chronic pain, and my bisexuality,' they explained to me over Twitter.

Have you ever considered that your parents could be bi? Or ace? Or gay? Or trans? I certainly hadn't. In all the confusion and stress of growing up, developing, and discovering our queerness, we tend to assume that the grown-ups in our life have it all figured out and the identity they present to the world (or that we've assumed they are projecting) is who they really are. For some bi parents, coming out is a way of demonstrating to their children that they shouldn't make assumptions, and challenging the monosexism that's engrained in all of us from a young age.

If these last few paragraphs don't apply to you because your parent/s are openly queer, treat yourself for reading them anyway by listening to some Lizzo.

BI THE WAY
So I originally came out when I was 18, in my first semester at university, via a drunk tweet that said 'I'm drunk, I'm

queer, and I have doughnut children'. I had no memory of doing this until the next morning when my Mutti asked me what my tweet was about and I was like 'well... I'm not straight' and she was really chill about it. But the people I was living with at uni were less okay about it so I found myself backing into a corner and denying my attraction to people of same-similar genders. So I spent a year exclusively dating and sleeping with people of different genders to my own, but I always knew something wasn't right and I was denying part of myself.

Then at the end of my second year of university, I started to date my now ex-girlfriend and so many people accused me of 'now being a lesbian' to the point that I internalized this and identified as a lesbian for 3.5 years. Because bisexuality is just a stepping stone to coming out as gay, right? So during the time I was in this relationship, the majority of my family (all but two members, my Mutti and my sister) disowned me for being queer; because it's something they believe I should be ashamed of, that I shouldn't exist, that I'm somehow less human for finding same-similar genders attractive. This year I moved to Brighton and started dating a man for the first time in over 4 years (which only lasted a few months), and people's reactions to me 'suddenly being straight' was hard to handle. It was a complete invalidation of all my prior relationships, all my potential future relationships, which is why I've now become so vocal about my bisexuality, about the fluidity of attraction, about the experience of attraction beyond gender. In the time since I've come to terms with my queerness as a bisexual, I've come to realize that I prefer to date and be involved with people of same-similar genders but that doesn't negate the potential for my attraction to people of different genders, regardless of what my homophobic family and the 'friends' I thought would support me would like to believe (and argue about behind my back).

Meg Murphy, bi+ activist

Double discrimination

The final reason for lower coming-out rates within the bi community is double discrimination. Double discrimination refers to the rejection, prejudice, and violence that bi people face from both straight and gay communities. Much like the findings from the 'It May Not "Get Better" for Bisexual Teens' study (ScienceDaily 2013), double discrimination has been shown to have a big impact on bi people's desire and ability to come out. Whereas gay men and lesbians are much less likely to experience prejudice and rejection from within the LGBTQIA+ community, this is a common experience for bisexual people. As a result of double discrimination, bi people are more likely to report feeling as though LGBTQIA+ people are not accepted in society, so it makes sense that people who already feel less accepted and more likely to face to face discrimination are less likely to come out. The Movement Advancement Project (MAP) explains:

Research is beginning to uncover the extent of this bias against bisexual people. For example, in a survey of bisexual people in 2013, nearly one in three bisexual people said that there is little to no acceptance of LGBT people in the United States today, compared to only 15% of gay men and 16% of lesbians. When asked about social acceptance for different groups within the

LGBT community, 33% LGBT people said there was a lot of social acceptance of bisexual women, compared to only 8% who said there was a lot of social acceptance for bisexual men. Finally, only 41% of bisexual people said that society is more accepting of people who are LGBT compared to 10 years ago. Sixty-six percent of gay men and 57% of lesbians said the same. (MAP 2016, p.5)

As an activist, I find myself getting so angry and frustrated when I read these stats. This research has been readily available for over a decade, yet no mainstream LGBTQIA+ organization has run any kind of campaign or created support systems to combat the isolation facing bi+ youth. It has been left to less-funded bi-specific orgs like the Bisexual Resource Center and Still Bisexual, who have first-hand experience of what double discrimination can feel like.

Knowing that if you come out you will not only face homophobia/biphobia from straight people but also the possibility of biphobia/rejection/aggression from other queer people can be incredibly intimidating and disheartening. As I wrote in an article for bi.org, 'What It's Like to Be Out But Not Out-Out as a Bisexual' (Shearing 2017), 'If you can't exist safely within heteronormative society, as bisexuals can't, the thought that you can't come in from the cold into queer spaces is terrifying.'

Despite this, thousands of bi+ people come out in their own capacities and live open, genuine, and authentic lives. Through their connections with the queer communities and their own queer identities, they makes friends, build chosen-families, and fall in love. On that note, let's move on to one of the chapter topics I'm most excited for: *What it's like dating while bi?*

CHAPTER 5

What's Dating Like for Bi People?

You might have heard this old saying: 'bisexuality immediately doubles your chances for a date on Saturday night'. But most bi people will tell you this is bullshit.

Biphobic stereotypes and prejudices

In fact, a lot of people find that being openly bi has actually limited their dating pool because of people's biphobic stereotypes and prejudices. Some of the most common and pervasive stereotypes about bi people are to do with dating and relationships, and how our multi-gender attractions make us subpar partners. You might have heard of these common tropes:

- Bi people are more likely to cheat because they can't be satisfied with just one gender.
- Bi people can't be monogamous (again, because we can't be satisfied with just one gender).
- Bi people can't settle down and will always leave you (for someone of a different gender to you).

Not only are these stereotypes about bi people incorrect, they also demonize traits like non-monogamy and promiscuity. They are also not applied in the same way to all bi people. For example, black bi women are much more likely to be stereotyped as sexually aggressive and insatiable, due to fetishization of both their race and sexuality. We will discuss this in more detail in the chapter on biphobia.

These stereotypes are so common and deeply ingrained in monosexual people that it isn't uncommon to hear people proudly proclaim that they simply don't date bisexuals! Unfortunately, this mindset isn't just found in straight people (although that would be bad enough); it is depressingly common among gay men and lesbians as well. As the Queer news outlet *them.* explained in an article called 'A New Study Explains Why Many Lesbians Are Biased Against Bisexual Women':

> Bisexual women, in particular, have it hard – at least when it comes to desirability within the LGBTQ+ community. Lesbian women and communities are notorious for rejecting bisexual women as potential friends and as sexual and romantic partners due to stereotypes that bisexual women are untrustworthy, unreliable, incapable of monogamy, disease carriers, and 'sleeping with the enemy'. Bisexual men are also stigmatized by gay men to some extent, but given gay men's lesser cultural emphasis on monogamy and greater interest in casual sex, bisexual men's desirability is less affected by these stereotypes, and may even be bolstered by gay men's preference for masculinity (which is perceived as higher among bisexual guys). (Vrangalova n.d.)

Countless amounts of ink, screen space, and airtime have been (rightfully) dedicated to busting these harmful myths, but let's get into them a bit anyway.

All of these tropes have a common theme: that being multi-gender attracted means that we as bi people can never be happy with just one person. It's been said to me and lots of other people that 'bisexuals just want to have their cake and eat it too', to which I say '*Of course* we do! What the hell else would you do with cake? The whole *point* of a cake is to eat it? What are the rest of you doing with your cakes?!'

The little kernel of insecurity at the centre of these stereotypes, the little bit of sand that gets into monosexual people's shells until they have to coat it in a big shiny pearl of biphobia, is the worry about not being enough. None of us wants to feel like we aren't good enough, like there's something we lack. We all want to feel like we could fill someone's cup of desires and needs until it's overflowing. For many people, multi-gender attracted people's cup seems much bigger and harder to fill, because there seems to be so much more possibility of what we could want.

BI THE WAY

I've had two relationships with women in the last few years after many years of dating only men and then realizing I was bi. For some reason I put way more expectations on these relationships so when things didn't end in a long-term relationship I put it down to me not being 'a good bi' or doubting my attraction/feelings towards women. I have so much more shyness and awkwardness around women but hey that's internalized biphobia and high expectations of self (thanks mind!). I think the women I dated had some of that shyness so more compassion and communication are on my lessons learned!

Kim

It's easier, then, to lash out at the very concept of bisexuality than to consider that maybe you weren't enough for someone you liked. It's easier to say 'that's just what bi girls do: they end up with men eventually' than to consider that maybe you weren't a good partner, or right for each other, or that simple truth we all face at least once: they just liked someone else more.

So when I hear people say 'I don't date bisexuals', I don't hear it as any kind of criticism of those who like a little bit of everything but more as a confession of insecurity: that the person cannot cope with the idea of being rejected or not enough, that they'd rather shut down any potential relationships with a huge range of people than face up to that insecurity.

Like the propensity to cheat, leave relationships, or have issues around commitment, etc., being non-monogamous is a personal choice/trait and is not linked to someone's sexuality. Our heteronormative society has vilified non-straight sexualities by associating them with supposedly negative traits like promiscuity and non-monogamy. So the stereotype of being promiscuous is not unique to bi people, but we do experience it from partners and potential partners in a way that other sexually identified people don't. Historically, these negative stereotypes arose from a time when same-sex relationships were illegal, forcing lovers into the shadows and a culture of anonymous, fleeting sexual encounters – known as cruising culture – developed among gay and bi men. Often, these men would have wives at home, either as cover or because they genuinely loved them, but were only able to express their same-gender desire in these illicit trysts. From here, we get the root of the stereotype of bisexual men being cheaters, abandoning their wives, or worse, spreading HIV to them. Whilst it's important to acknowledge where these stereotypes have come from, that doesn't make them acceptable or reasonable, even at the time.

The final stereotype is that bi people will always leave same-gender relationships to be in 'straight-passing', different-gender relationships. Bi women in particular face this stereotype, often being accused of being 'lesbians until graduation', i.e. bi women are only interested in dating women when they are young and 'experimenting', but will choose or end up settling down with men for the assumed safety of heteronormativity. As the stereotype goes, it's therefore pointless to attempt to date us because our hearts aren't really in the whole 'queer relationship' thing and we'll just leave our same-gender partners anyway. Because obviously, something is only meaningful and worthwhile if it's permanent and someone leaving you for a person of a different gender is way worse than them leaving you for any other reason.

There's a Pew Research LGBT Survey from 2013 that is often quoted online to 'back up' gay people's reservations about dating bi people, which suggests that over 80 per cent of bi people end up in different-gender relationships (Marusic 2016). First, so what if we do? What if blond people were more likely to date other blond people? Does that mean it would make sense to write off the possibility of dating blonds if you have a different hair colour? Would you claim that all blonds end up with other blonds eventually, even if you met a blond who really liked you and wanted to be with you? Second, by the time you're reading this book, that study will most likely be nearly or over a decade old. A lot of things change in that time, particularly in terms of acceptance and visibility of LGBTQIA+ people. Remember those statistics about how quickly the number of people identifying as LGBTQIA+ (especially bi) are rising? I bet that study would look different now, as there are more queer people, making it easier and statistically more likely to find or be in a same-gender relationship.

BI THE WAY

I came out to my partner about a year and a half ago. She seemed to take it well enough – unlike my mother, who wondered why I couldn't 'stick to one gender'. But after half a year or so, during a small argument, she revealed her fear that I was going to leave her for a man. After all, why would I tell her I was bi if that was not my intention? I was shocked to hear this from the person I loved most, and it really gave me perspective on how little most people know about bi people. We had to sit down and have a long talk to address her stereotypes about bi people. No, I do not want to cheat just because I'm bi; No, I am not 50/50 man/woman (though some are, I'm sure); No, I am not unable to be monogamous (though if that's not your thing, get it!); and No, I did not love her less because of it. Thankfully, we managed to move past it and are now happy together, but this episode really opened my eyes to how little people know about bi people; how we're, or at least I'm, not magical unicorns but the same as everyone else. To all the young bis, growing up in this more accepting era: know that *acceptance* is not *understanding*. There's still a way to go in that department, and non-bi people hold a lot of stereotypes that can impact your relationship negatively. So it comes to each and every one of us to spread the word that like all the gays and straights and aros/aces, we're one sprawling humanity. We love who we love, and we are who we are, with our own flaws and strengths. But be prepared to face misunderstanding from straights and gays alike, and try to eliminate these as early as you can in a relationship, lest you want headaches and years

> of trouble. What seems obvious to us is not obvious to
> many others.
>
> *Anonymous*

When I posted that I was writing about this trope on Twitter (and how frustrated I was about reading explanations from people who refused to date bi partners), a lot of my bi followers chimed in with their own experiences of being rejected for their bisexuality. Bi advocate Thomas Leavitt pointed out to me on Twitter:

> That attitude is a total disregard for the basic math of the available relationship possibilities that leads to this. There are simply many more opportunities to date differently gendered partners. With regards to bi women, this is aggravated by biphobia in significant chunks of the lesbian world, and by the fact that the many bi women in same gender relationships are often read as lesbians. Bi men deal with biphobia as well, so we tend to date other bi+ people as a survival mechanism...and since most of us are closeted, that means that the bulk of our potential bi+ partners are women, who also tend to see us as more compatible than cishet men.

Others mentioned how being threatened by a potential partner's bisexuality certainly isn't restricted to any one gender or sexuality. While some gay men and lesbians may be more vocal about their outright rejection of us, even straight people who are (perceived to be, at least) more willing to take a bi partner may be fostering biphobic views that can lead to possessiveness, increased jealousy, antagonistic comments, etc. So even if a person is willing to *date* a bi person, that still doesn't necessarily mean they *accept* bi people.

Unfortunately because of this, studies have shown that bi+ women in relationships with men are more likely to face domestic violence after coming out, suggesting that biphobia can be a possible motivator (Frieden et al. 2018; Johnson and Grove 2017). It's important to note when we explore how some minorities experience higher rates of sexual violence that their minority identity (bisexual/disabled/ethnic minority/etc.) is not to blame. Someone is not abused because they are part of a minority; they are abused because an abuser or violent person weaponizes their minority status against them. The difference may seem small, but it's important that we shift our language away from blaming the victim, even in subtle ways, to acknowledging how abusive or violent people will prey on minorities, as they are less likely to be taken seriously. We'll discuss this much further in the chapter about biphobia (see Chapter 7).

Coming out when going out

Coming out to (potential) partners or dates is another struggle that bi+ people face. As we've already explored, it's often assumed that people going on dates with people of a different gender to them are straight, and people going on same-gender dates are gay. This means that bi people have to make a decision as to whether to come out to their date or partner. People approach this in different ways: lots of bi people choose to have their sexuality in their dating profiles to help screen out people with biphobic views (this can backfire, which we'll discuss in a sec); others come out once the relationship has gotten off the ground and they feel like they can fully trust their partners; and some don't ever tell their partner. Through my work as the founder of the Bi Survivors Network, I've spoken to lots of people who are still closeted to their husband or wife of multiple years. Usually, these people who confess their sexuality in the privacy of the BSN Direct Messages are men, usually middle-aged or older. While this is far from a conclusive study, this anecdotal evidence does align with the statistics that show that bi men are very unlikely to be out. Deciding to come out to your date or partner is completely up to you; you don't owe coming out to anyone, even your partner. If you do choose to, make sure you're doing it out of a feeling of safety and trust. While it can be scary, lots of bi people find that coming out to their partner is a very positive experience; it can lead to a better connection as you can be your full, authentic self with your partner. Also, if you find you don't trust your partner or date enough to come out to them, consider if this is someone you really want to be with. You should feel safe and comfortable to be your true, complete self with the person you love.

Having your sexuality on your dating profile (if you have one) can be a good way to screen out biphobic people. On the flip side, lots of people on dating sites and apps who have done this have also found themselves being approached for threesomes, even if they have no interest in them, which is a type of sexual harassment. 'Unicorn hunting' is the term used to describe a different-gender couple who are looking for a single bi woman to join them for a threesome. The 'unicorn' part of 'unicorn hunting' refers to how rare bi women who want to have threesomes with a couple that already have an intimate relationship are. Unfortunately, this experience isn't just limited to people on dating sites and apps; being asked for threesomes when someone finds out you're bi is a pretty common experience and has become the source of a lot of frustration and memes in the bi+ community. Once while I was still in college, I was waiting at the bus stop with a boy I briefly dated in secondary school and a friend of his whom I didn't know. Somehow, my sexuality came up in conversation – I don't remember exactly how, I think my ex was bragging to his friend or his friend had asked if I was gay now because of my short hair and androgynous style (because that's how that works). The friend then said to my ex, 'Why did you break up with her before getting a threesome? That's what they're good for.' I felt pretty embarrassed and used the crowded bus as an excuse to sit away from them.

It's also important to note that wanting to have threesomes or be a unicorn doesn't make you a bad bi, or mean you are encouraging others to unicorn hunt. You are allowed to express your sexuality however you want, and others should have enough respect to understand that just because some bi people like threesomes doesn't mean all bi people do. As activist Robyn Ochs says: 'You are not responsible for the bi brand' (Zane 2017).

BI THE WAY

Well firstly, there's the ever common coming out to a partner and them suggesting if you ever wanted a threesome, ya know, they would be down if you wanted to explore that part of your sexuality. And by partner I mean those of the male variety, in that case. But I think the worst date I've ever had was this girl, it was my first official date with a woman, and she came on so strong even though I had said I'm reserved and not a very sexual person. She 'jokingly' said why are you checking her out when a woman in heels walked by. I was genuinely just turning towards the noise. But I just didn't know what to say, it was so aggressive and

was said within ten minutes of meeting her. Still waiting
on a positive all-around dating experience, people don't
really understand grey demibisexuals, 'cause they just
assume bisexuals are this super sexual being, but I'm in
chronic pain, I ain't got the energy or the want.

Lolo

The dating pool is becoming a dating ocean

But things are getting better. As more and more people identify
as bi, pan, queer, gay, not-straight, etc., the dating pool for all
of us really is expanding and becoming more welcoming. 'I feel
like as I get older I'm experiencing less and less stereotypes/dis-
crimination for my identity,' Zachary Zane, bisexual influencer
and sex writer, explains to me over email. 'I think that's partly
because more millennials are identifying somewhere on the bi+
spectrum and there has been so much more bi+ visibility in the
media. But still, I've run into the issue of gay men not wanting
to date me because they're afraid I'll choose a less resistant path
of being in a 'straight' relationship. (Obviously the relationship
isn't straight since I'm queer, but that's what they call opposite-
sex relationships.) And since the majority of bi men end up in
"straight" relationships, they fear that I'll leave them for a woman.
This is unequivocally wrong,' he tells me.

Zach's article 'The Silver Lining of Dating When Bi' (Zane
2016) on bi.org also has some great examples of some of the perks
of dating bi people. I particularly like the third point Zach raises
in that blog: 'they're [bi partners] probably not super heteronormative'. Bi people are often accused of being 'traitors to the cause'

of gay liberation or choosing 'a comfortable heteronormative lifestyle' if we are in long-term relationships that 'look straight' (and I hope by now you agree with me that relationships don't have orientations and you shouldn't make assumptions about relationships based on how they look). But people don't stop being bi once we're in relationships, monogamous or not, meaning that the way we approach relationships is influenced by our queer experiences and identities. This means that bi people in different-gender relationships may approach these in ways that two straight people may not. For example, we may be more likely to reject gender roles and expectations. This is just one of the reasons I reject the accusation that bi people uphold or play into heteronormative ideas by being in different-gender relationships. The other reason is that this is often a bad-faith accusation and is like the allegation that bisexuality 'reinforces the gender binary', and we should always question who is and isn't being accused and why.

A friend once joked to me that her and her (now ex-)boyfriend had 'become a little too heteronormative' as they were monogamous and lived together. I completely relate to the feeling of losing touch with part of your queer identity when you're in a different-gender relationship (and this same feeling has been expressed by a lot of bi+ people), but disagree that her relationship is in any way contributing to heteronormativity. First, both her and her boyfriend are openly bi, thereby pushing back against the idea that everyone is straight, and she is a fierce feminist activist who does a lot of campaigning around queer issues and relationships and consent. In the same way, lots of bi people who are openly themselves while in different-gender relationships are helping to fight against the cultural assumption that everyone is straight.

Bi-tinted glasses

Previously I've described this as 'seeing life through bi-tinted glasses' or approaching relationships and dating, regardless of genders, 'through a lens of queerness'. Most people still seem to view bisexuality as a switch that flips between 'attracted to a man' and 'attracted to a woman', which not only ignores all other genders but also fails to capture the way our multi-gender attraction affects the way we are attracted to people of different genders. So, for example, a woman being attracted to and dating a man still makes decisions about pursuing that man and decisions in that relationship that are informed by her other desires and experiences with queerness. In my opinion, this is why bi women's attraction to men is not the same as straight women's (same for bi men), and this is also why bi people's different-gender relationships aren't necessarily a product or pillar of heteronormativity.

Making a conscious choice to approach desires and relationships with men/women/enbies in the same way and to hold partners to the same standards regardless of gender is the basis of bi feminism, which we discussed a bit in the chapter on gender (see Chapter 3) and will discuss further in the coming chapters. Not all bi people are consciously bi feminists, or even striving to hold partners to the same standard regardless of gender, but I do believe that all bi people's desires and relationships are influenced by our experiences of being queer and multi-gender attracted, whether that manifests as bi feminism or even just as taking small steps to stay in touch with your queerness/bi-ness while in monogamous relationships. Whether this is as simple as wearing 'still bisexual' pins, refusing to let your identity be erased, being involved in LGBTQIA+ activism, or even being closeted, these actions mean the relationship will be a markedly different experience than a monosexual person might have in a similar-looking partnership.

BI THE WAY

Coming out as bi to partners has been historically awful. I told my first real boyfriend and he outed me to all of his friends shortly after, which was like, woah, private conversation. A more typical response from cis men is them being delighted because that means we could have a threesome. And they genuinely think that's a statement of support when it just tells me what they think they'll gain from my identity. And really, it prevents them connecting with that part of my identity in any real way. I had a one-night stand where he was just like, 'that's cool I don't mind', which made it seem like I was asking his permission to be bisexual.

One time I went on a date with a guy and he followed me on insta so then he's on the date like, 'So you're bi right?'... I'm like yeah it's literally all over my Instagram where you follow me. And then he proceeded to ask a series of problematic and incredibly personal questions. He's like, 'Do you typically have a boyfriend and a girlfriend? Would you have a threesome with me? How did your parents react to you coming out?' I was like, woah, INTENSE.

Dating someone of a similar gender for the first time was really intense because 1) it's an entirely different relationship dynamic a lot of the time. And 2) I think I put a lot of pressure on the relationship to work because it had taken me so long to accept myself enough to date women. And I conflated that with it taking a long time to find that particular woman. So it was hard to imagine I'd find another woman ever again. I think I'm a lot better at dating now that I'm more secure with my bisexuality. And of course, I also date non-binary people and doing that the first time really shifted my perceptions of sexuality, beauty, and gender.

Lastly, dating a fellow bi person was dope in a lot of ways – someone who understands my sexuality – but also drudged up some internalized biphobia I had which was not dope. Like she dated a guy after me and I caught myself thinking, 'Maybe she's not really bi.' And I just hated myself lmao. I was like how could I think that? Terrible. She's def bi, and that moment of weakness was like the deepest darkest thoughts I ever had in my life. But I immediately caught myself and corrected myself.

Gabriel Alexa, sex writer, bi activist,
and founder of Bi Girls Club

Like those in different-gender relationships, bi people in same/similar-gender relationships also find our identities being erased. This happens in (at least) two ways for bi people in either same- or different-gender relationships: one is the good old-fashioned assumption that bi people 'choose a side' and become either gay or straight when we settle into relationships, and the other is that our relationships are labelled as being either lesbian/gay or straight regardless of whether anyone in the relationship actually identifies that way. I personally don't believe that relationships have an orientation and labelling my relationships as either gay/lesbian or straight suggests that those monosexual labels have more weight than my own bisexual label. This, for me, plays into the commonly held belief that monosexual identities are more real and stable than non-monosexual ones; that they are the inevitable, fixed end-point of sexuality. When I've expressed this sentiment before, people have asked me how I describe my relationships. I just call it my 'relationships'. If people want clarity as to my partner's gender, they can ask. For me, this is a small step I can take to make people challenge their assumptions about couplings. But I also understand that, for others, there is empowerment to be found in calling their relationships gay/lesbian/straight or even queer. For that reason, I advocate not labelling other people's relationships, especially not in the media, but to let people do so themselves if they so wish.

Otherwise, always referring to relationships as gay/lesbian or straight in the media (well, let's be honest, it's only same-gender relationships that are ever deemed to need a qualifier as different gender. Assumed straight relationships are considered the default) contributes to an environment of monosexism, where everyone is assumed to be gay or straight until stated otherwise. Think of all the headlines proclaiming that celebrities are 'now in a lesbian/gay relationship' once they start publicly dating someone of the same gender, even if they are out as bi. How many people reading those headlines will stop to think about how the people in that relationship identify, compared to how many will assume that anyone in a 'gay/lesbian relationship' must be gay/lesbian? In the same way, most people will assume that public figures in different-gender relationships are straight as a default regardless of whether their relationship is labelled as such, but labelling relationships as gay/lesbian still contributes to bi erasure and monosexism.

One notable example is that of bi activist Robyn Ochs, who was one of the first people in the state of Massachusetts to enter into a same-sex marriage. Robyn and her wife Peg Preble were fervent campaigners for equal marriage, as well as Robyn being a well-known bisexual activist and founder of several bi organizations in the state. Somewhat ironically, Robyn was identified in the press on the event as a lesbian entering into a lesbian marriage. Even in a ten-year follow-up on the story, the journalist carefully avoids using the word 'bisexual'. Ochs and Preble's photo was used nationally and they were labelled a lesbian couple repeatedly, even by *The Washington Post*, to which they gave an exclusive interview headlined, 'A Carefully Considered Rush to the Altar: Lesbian Pair Wed After 7 Years Together'. 'The pair quickly became poster children for "gay marriage",' Eliel Cruz (2014) wrote for *them*, in an article about the erasure of bisexuality in the coverage of same-sex marriage. In the same piece, Robyn explained what this meant to her:

> To me personally, it matters because one of the challenges of identifying as bisexual is dealing with repeated erasure. My identity is hard-won – I worked very hard and for a very long time to come to a place of comfort and pride about who I am, and it matters to me that people see me accurately.

Bi people have been falling in love, settling down, and even getting married for as long as gay and straight people. So let's explore a little more of our history in the next chapter, including some historical bi lovers.

CHAPTER 6

How Long Has Bisexuality Been Around?

For as long as there have been humans, there have been humans who were attracted to multiple genders. In every phase of history, every civilization, every part of the world has been chock-full of people who today might identify as bi/pan/queer/etc. The same is true for gay men, lesbians, trans, non-binary, and asexual people, and every other flavour of queerness there is (which is infinite, in my opinion).

There are a few different ways you can approach the vastness of bi history. You can reach back through the archives and find people who had relationships or showed attractions to different genders across their lives and claim them as bi. You can focus only on people who actually identified themselves as bi. You can look into the ways in which bi people have been pathologized and ostracized by others. You can focus just on the many, *many* achievements of bi community groups and organizations.

In true bi fashion, I'm interested in a bit of everything. While I think it can be problematic to anachronistically apply modern labels to figures for whom those identities may not have existed, I also understand the importance of acknowledging the queerness of our ancestors, icons, and enemies. By that I mean that we can and should acknowledge and shout about historical figures who appeared to be multi-gender attracted, but it's also important to be aware that throughout most of history, queerness was forcibly erased and invisibilized, meaning people may not have fully been able to comprehend or express their own experiences.

People who may appear to us as bi may have actually identified as gay or ace or any number of other identities if they had access to our words and knowledge. If you look back through history, there are countless people who could have fitted into multiple of today's identities and there are just as many arguments about which they 'truly' were. I find those arguments to be a waste of time because we can never know – they do nothing but sow seeds of division within our community, and perpetuate the idea that queer identities and experiences can always be neatly separated from each other and don't overlap. In today's world, Sappho, the famous poet from Lesbos, may have identified as a lesbian, or bi, or pan, or even something completely different. But she didn't have access to any of those words, and trying to claim her as definitely one or the other deprioritizes all the ways in which our experiences as lesbians or bi or pan women overlap and look like one another. She is an important figure to all women who love women, and that's all that matters to me.

With that in mind, then, this whistle-stop tour of bi history will comprise three parts: pre-bi history (i.e. multi-gender attracted people and communities that existed before our understanding of the word 'bisexual'), the emergence of bisexuality as a defined experience and community, and, finally, the bisexual movement from its inception in the '70s until now (I'm writing in 2021, remember).

BI THE WAY

It's important for bi+ people to document our history because otherwise we risk losing records of our community and activism, which not only allows biphobic people to continue to argue that we don't exist, are a new concept, or don't have a community or history, but also means that bi people won't have an awareness of the history of their community and the work of other bi people. Having a sense of history and community can be really important to understanding yourself and I know for myself learning that bi+ people have existed for as long as anything else and have made significant contributions as activists to the LGBTQ+ community was really important.

It can be difficult to find information about historical people who had relationships with or attraction to people of the same and different gender because historians and researchers only see heterosexual and gay/lesbian identities as an option. There can also be a misconception that it's anachronistic to identify people who had relationships with or experienced attraction to people of the same and different genders as part of bisexual+ history, and that it detracts from gay and lesbian history – however I feel very strongly that we have a right to acknowledge our community's heritage and that it only adds to the wider LGBTQ+ heritage.

I really expected more people to feel like my research was kind of 'treading on the toes' of gay and lesbian history and initially I felt a little defensive about what I was doing. I've gradually realized that maintaining a positive, inclusive space with the @bihistory Instagram, workshops, and the archive collection itself has had the same positive energy returned to it, and I've had many people reach out and give feedback to say that it's helped them feel more comfortable in their identities and given them a sense of heritage which is really important.

Mel Reeve, bi+ archivist

Proto-bisexuality

Mary Wollstonecraft is often called a 'proto-feminist' because, whilst she was a dedicated women's rights activist, feminism as a political movement or defined ideology/framework had not yet been established at the time of her writing. 'Bisexuality' as a concept and identity has a specific context; it relies on a certain understanding of gender, attraction (see Chapters 1 and 2), and sexuality. Our concept of bisexuality began to emerge in the late 1800s, alongside society's understanding (or, misunderstanding might be more accurate) of hetero- and homosexuality. But this didn't stop people from desiring, loving, and fucking people of all different genders!

The ancient world was full of practices and people who we would perhaps now label as bisexual. In ancient Greece, it was not uncommon for free men to have relationships with women and younger men. Interestingly, this became a more common – or at least a more open – part of life after Greece became a city-state. Eva Cantarella writes in *Bisexuality in the Ancient World*:

After Sappho, in Greece, love between women was no longer the subject of poetry. How could it have been any different, when one considers that with the strengthening of the bonds of citizenship, women had been relegated to a reproductive role, excluded from all forms for education, and consequently from the use of language? In the centuries of the city-state, female homosexuality disappeared as a socially visible and significant custom. And at the same time, male homosexuality came out, as a manner of speaking. (2002, p.4)

It should be noted here that Eva uses 'homosexual' to refer to any and all same-sex/gender desire or relationships, which strikes me as a bit ironic in a book about bisexuality.

The practice of men having relationships with younger men was known as 'pederasty', and it is arguable that pederasty was more common than bisexuality, as boys were seen as having a status closer to women than to men, meaning men engaging with younger *boys* was not seen as on a par with engaging sexually with other *men*. It's important to note that many of these relationships would have been predatory, and even considered paedophilia today.

Around a similar time, bisexuality was also seemingly in vogue in another Mediterranean climate: in ancient Rome, it was considered permissible for a freeborn man to have sex with men and women, provided he always took the penetrative role. This seems to have been the ancient Roman version of 'no-homo'ing their relationships with other men, in the same way that today we see frat boys claim that sucking each other off isn't 'gay' because it was part of an initiation.

It is interesting to see how in both these cultures the binary applied to sexuality was not gender but rather penetrating/being penetrated as a way of determining who was the active/strong/dominant party or the passive/weak/submissive participant in a way that we still see applied to gender roles today (see Chapter 2 for a deeper exploration of this). Same shit, different centuries.

Some notable Greco-Romans who dabbled in multi-gender flings include Socrates, the Greek philosopher, who was married to a 'difficult woman' but had an eye for beautiful boys, especially his student Alcibiades, and Julius Caesar, who, despite being married, bedded both Cleopatra and King Nicomedes.

Ancient Japan also saw its fair share of bisexuality and homosexuality among Buddhists monks, with many stories of same-sex love affairs appearing in countless literary works. Monks were also the first people to rationalize pederasty in Japan.

The violent spread of Christian morality during the Dark Ages meant any hint of queerness and gender non-conformity has been erased and suppressed in the pages of history and possibly at the time too. But nothing can or will ever stamp it out, and multi-gender attracted people continue to love and exist.

One of my favourite examples is playwright William Shakespeare, who, long before becoming the bane of every school child's life, was writing sonnets for his paramours of varying genders and infusing his plays with tales of gender-bending and queer love. Willy Shake is also one of my favourite examples of bi erasure, as one theory posits that 'he' was actually several people writing under the same pseudonym, so the sonnets written for women were by men and vice versa.

There were several other notable people who showed bisexual behaviour before 'bi' became the identity as we know it today, including (but certainly not limited to): Michelangelo, Casanova, Marie Antoinette, Lord Byron, Hans Christian Anderson, Alexander Hamilton, Virginia Woolf, Marlene Dietrich, Eleanor Roosevelt, Greta Garbo, Billie Holiday, Josephine Baker, Frida Kahlo, Edna St. Vincent Millay, Aleister Crowley, Colette, Francis Bacon, Tallulah Bankhead, Tamara de Lempicka, Mary Wollstonecraft, and many, many, many others.

The emergence of bi identities

As we discussed in Chapter 3, the word 'bisexual' was first used to describe people we might now describe as intersex before becoming used to describe people who have relationships with 'both sexes' at around the turn of the 20th century and then being popularized (not necessarily in positive or helpful ways) by sexologists and writers Freud, Kinsey, and Klein. For a while there was a flurry of activity in the sexologist world, attempting to prove – or more aptly disprove – the existence of multi-gender attraction and desire, but it was still minute compared to studies and theories on hetero- and homosexuality. 'When we began our investigation ten years ago, almost nothing was known about bisexuality. Even today, we are struck by the virtual absence of research on people attracted erotically to people of both sexes especially in light of research that suggests that bisexuality is fairly widespread,' wrote Weinberg, Pryor, and Williams in 1994, at the beginning of their fascinating multi-year study of bisexual lives in San Francisco. Sadly, not much has changed.

Meanwhile, multi-gender attracted people were hard at work toiling in the ranks of gay liberation, and queer and lesbian rights movements. Some were out as bi, whether proudly, reluctantly, or apologetically, whereas others didn't or couldn't label their sexuality and some identified as gay or lesbian either due to political pressure, or confusion, or many other reasons, before coming out as bi once the bi movement gained momentum.

One such figure was Stephen Donaldson, aka Donny the Punk (born Robert Anthony Martin Jr, he adopted the pseudonym to avoid embarrassing his father with his gay antics and in honour of the first man he loved, who was called Donald). In 1966, inspired by friends of his then-boyfriend, Donny founded the Student Homophile League at Columbia University, where he was studying. The group went on to become America's first student gay rights group and the first known LGBT students' movement. The chartering of the group caused quite a media storm and brought a lot of unfavourable attention to Columbia University and Donny. In the course of the two years after its inception and being chartered, Donny had fallen in love with a woman named Judith Jones and began identifying as bisexual.

In 1969, activist Brenda Howard organized the Christopher Street Liberation Day March a month after the riots at the Stonewall Inn and another a year later to mark the anniversary, and, luckily for us, the tradition stuck. So Brenda, a polyamorous bisexual Jewish kinkster, who eventually married a man, became known as the Mother of Pride. She was a prolific organizer. Before the Christopher Street Liberation Day March, she was a founding chairperson of the Gay Activists Alliance. She was arrested multiple times throughout the '80s and '90s for protesting and organized many events for the leather community.

Ten years later, ABilly Jones-Hennin, another bisexual, was creating the DC–Baltimore Coalition of Black Gays (now known as the DC Coalition) before going on to found the first national African American gay activist group, The National Coalition of Black Lesbians and Gays. He was an active member of organizing the March on Washington for Gay and Lesbian Rights in 1979. ABilly played a vital role in fighting for the inclusion of African Americans in the early gay liberation movement and ensuring that the issues and concerns of black Americans were included in the AIDS activism of the time.

There are so many more. In every chapter of every gay liberation group, in every lesbian feminist circle, in every gay students' alliance, in every protest, reading circle, and gay and lesbian support centre, we were there. We were raising funds, we were organizing new chapters and sitting on subcommittees, we were getting arrested, we were manning hotlines, and we were bringing snacks to meetings. Our names may have gone unwritten or misidentified, but have no doubt about it: we were everywhere.

The bi movement

At the beginning of the '70s, some of the bi people working their butts off for the gay and lesbian rights movement started to get a bit sick and tired of all the biphobia they were enduring while doing it. Some of it was overt and some of it was a subtle dismissal of multi-gender attracted people's experiences and issues, but all of it got under their skin.

At the beginning of the '70s, Donny the Punk had just been thrown out of the Navy for sleeping with men. He had entered the service after leaving the gay liberation movement due to the biphobia he'd encountered. 'As a bisexual no longer feeling comfortable in the gay liberation movement, I found myself in June, 1972, attending the annual Friends (Quakers) General conference in Ithaca, New York; its theme for the year was "Where Should Friends Be Pioneering Now?"' wrote Donny in a reflective essay which appears in *Bisexual Politics: Theories, Queries, and Visions* (Donaldson 1995, p.34). He found himself presenting a wildly impromptu workshop about bisexuality, which led to the creation of the Ithaca Statement on Bisexuality. 'The statement, which may have been the first public declaration of the bisexual movement, was printed in the Friends Journal (the FGC monthly), and the Advocate (thus announcing the bi consciousness to the gay world)' (p.34). Donny died of AIDS-related illnesses a year after the publication of the essay.

In 1972, the same year as the Ithaca Statement on Bisexuality was published, the National Bisexual Liberation Group formed in New York, possibly the first bi-specific organization. They began circulating the first bisexual newsletter, *The Bisexual Expression*, to over 5500 subscribers across the US.

Bi groups and communities proliferated in the US in the '70s. The year 1975 saw the formation of the Bi Forum in the US, followed in 1976 by the San Francisco Bisexual Community Center opening its doors for the first time. It went on to become the longest surviving community centre for bi+ people and the epicentre of much of the bi movement's advancement. It counted among its founders and volunteers such titans of the bi movement as Brenda Howard and Lani Ka'ahumanu. In a history of the Bay Area Bi+ and Pan Network, Lani explains:

> The groundbreaking, volunteer-run San Francisco Bisexual Center opened its doors on Hayes Street in 1976, offering support groups, counselling services, social events and a newsletter, and publicly aligned itself with the gay movement. In March 1983, as the reality of 'gay cancer' dawned, a small band of out bi activists within the lesbian and gay communities founded BiPOL, the first bisexual political action group in the USA. At the forefront of early sex-positive HIV/AIDS awareness and education programs, bi men and women were a driving force in what was to become the San Francisco Model. With the greater stigmatization of bisexuality and the increasing involvement of bi activists in HIV/AIDS prevention work, and bisexual men getting sick and dying the Center was drained of the volunteer energy necessary to keep it open, and shut its doors in 1984. (Ka'ahumanu and White 2002)

In order to help gain visibility for the group and to encourage others to join, Lani pulled possibly my favourite stunt in bi history and ran for Vice President of the United States in 1984. The plan was hatched by another BiPOL founder, Alan Rockway, who suggested Lani would make the most media-bait candidate because of her backstory as a heterosexual housewife who came out as gay and then later came out as bi. On the day of the Democratic National Convention (DNC), where Lani was hoping to address the convention and, more importantly, the television cameras, gay and lesbian Democrats had organized a march but told the bi group explicitly that they weren't welcome. However, the gay and lesbian Democrats forgot to provide any drinks, so attendants ended up flocking to BiPOL's pre-DNC rally, which was handing out ice water on that very hot day. 'It was important visibility. Even if it sounds completely silly, at the time there was nothing about bisexuality except the negative piece that we're spreading HIV/AIDS. If we're out there talking about more funding for AIDS, the Equal Rights Amendment or recognizing lesbian, gay and bisexual families, it addresses the issues,' Lani told KQED in 2020 (Voynovskaya 2020).

The 1980s were arguably the most important decade in LGBT-QIA+ history. 'The first bisexual organizations outside the United States developed in Europe in the 1980s. The London Bisexual Group was created by men involved in the anti-sexist men's movement in 1981. Bisexual organizations subsequently began in the Netherlands (1983), Scotland (1984), and West Germany (1984). The Netherlands group, the Dutch National Bi Network, is the oldest continuing bisexual organization in the world,' notes activist and writer Brett Genny Beemyn (2014, p.2) in a pamphlet on the bi+ movement. Although there were most certainly queer groups and groups that addressed the needs of bisexual people beyond America and the West before this, they just might not have made it into the West's official version of queer history.

This was also the decade when the AIDS crisis reached a

fever pitch, leading to a wave of hypervisibility for queer people. History and discourse around AIDS and the AIDS crisis often focus on gay men, but all members of the queer community were deeply affected, as were several other vulnerable and minority groups, including sex workers and drug addicts. The bi community was both deeply affected by and heavily involved in action against the AIDS crisis. Alexei Guren, the bisexual founder of Gay Teen Task Force (now PrideLines) in Florida, co-founded the Health Crisis Network in 1983 in order to provide a response to the growing crisis. Meanwhile, bi activists Dr David Lourea and Cynthia Slater were offering safer-sex workshops in bath houses and kink clubs in San Francisco. In 1985, Cynthia started the first Women's HIV/AIDS Information Switchboard. She died only four years later of AIDS-related illnesses.

Other bi activists were also heavily involved in the response. For example, Carol Leigh (aka Scarlot Harlot) was a founding member of ACT UP (AIDS Coalition to Unleash Power) in San Francisco, probably the best-known response group of the AIDS crisis. It would be impossible to list them all here, partly because there were so many and partly because often these activists, their identity, or their work are erased from the pages of history. 'Not only is the bi community not reaping the positive results of all their efforts to the same levels as the gay community, but we are not even acknowledged for our work and commitment, and, quite unbelievably, actually criticized for not being there! Adding insult to injury, the community is simultaneously chastised for not fighting hard enough for bisexual recognition and visibility,' writes author Harrie Farrow (2016) for bi.org on the topic of bi people's part in the gay civil rights movement and the accusation that bi people 'rode on gay men and lesbians' coattails' without actually being a part of the fight.

The '80s was also the decade when the bi+ movement began

to proliferate across Europe and the rest of the world. You might have noticed that this history of the bi+ movement has been pretty American-centric so far. There's a few key reasons for that: first, it seems that the first bi groups that did exist were American, as we've seen so far. Second, the history of the LGBTQIA+ movement is pretty American-centric, either because Western culture is in general or because Americans are just better at documenting their history and making it available. I think it's probably a bit of both.

The first BiCon, Britain's oldest bi+ conference, was held in 1984 in London. The theme of the Conference was 'The Politics of Bisexuality', and the attendees tasked themselves with creating a bisexual manifesto. In true bi fashion, they couldn't settle on only one, so they produced two.

'The "Second Politics of Bisexuality Conference" was also in London, at the London Lesbian and Gay Centre, in April 1985. Booked into London's new Lesbian and Gay Community Centre, the "lesbian sex wars" of the time meant that bisexual groups were banned from the Centre. (Their mere presence would oppress lesbians, apparently.)' explains Ian Watters, one of BiCon's co-founders, on BiCon's website. The conference has found several different homes since then and is one of the world's longest running bi+ conventions.

BI THE WAY

Since I was 12 I have been part of a niche music community, which has meant I have had friends much older than me. One such friend is an incredible whirlwind of a man who has been with the same man since the nineties. Considering this and his particular brand of flamboyant, it isn't surprising people generally refer to him as gay.

As a teen, I had the sort of hero-worship crush on him where I just wanted to be around him and listen to his stories whenever I could. I don't remember the context at all, but I so clearly remember when I was about 15 him telling a story about his days in the old London Lesbian and Gay Centre. He so casually talked about how he and a woman he met there dated for a bit and then got shunned from coming back because they were bi.

My feelings in response were such a complex thing. A huge chunk of 'oh wow, he's like me' combined with the downer of 'people like me aren't wanted in the community'. It's been maybe 16 years since he told me this story and I still remember that emotional mix so viscerally.

Emily January

During the same time that BiCon was fighting with the Lesbian and Gay Centre to be able to use the venue, a slightly less literal (but not in every case) version of the fight to be allowed and recognized under the rainbow umbrella alongside gay men and lesbians was happening across the Western world. Many bi activists began agitating and advocating for the 'B' to be added to 'LG', but not all bi activists agreed. Some argued that bisexuals should strive to create our own separate community, whereas others felt that being part of the gay and lesbian community was a better or enough of a political vantage point. For example, in her essay 'Why You Must Say "and Bisexual"', Nishanga Bliss writes:

If you look at the Kinsey studies with an inclusive eye, you find that 40% of the population is behaviorally bisexual. Bisexuals are working to organize these people to create a space for them to finally be safe, to come out in. Add that 40 to the 10% gay and lesbian population and you get 50% queer. If we don't rise up and take power then, when will we? The real fear, expressed in fear of bisexuals, is the fear that we queers have of our own power. (Bliss 1995, p.258)

However, in an essay published in the same anthology, *Bisexual Politics: Theories, Queries, and Visions*, Liz A. Highleyman argued that becoming part of the 'LesBiGay' community would erase bi+ specific issues. First, she explains:

Many gay/lesbian-identified bisexuals are not seeking inclusion as outsiders, but have long been a part of the gay and lesbian movement (sometimes before they identified as bi, sometimes as closeted bis); to them, the failure of gay men and lesbians to include bisexuals feels like exclusion or expulsion. Many bisexuals seek to take advantage of the size and infra structure of the gay and lesbian movement which many bisexuals helped to build. Within the gay and lesbian movement, bisexual activism is often centered around getting the word 'bisexual' included in group names and statements of purpose. (Highleyman 1995, p.83)

Before arguing:

It seems to me that trying to build a LesBiGay (or LesBiGayTrans) movement is misguided. If we want our issues as bisexuals to be addressed, we should build an independent bisexual movement and work in coalition with others when our concerns coincide. (p.85)

But as the tides of history show, the 'gay and lesbian community' eventually expanded in mainstream consciousness to become the slightly more accurate 'LGBTQIA+ community'. This didn't happen by accident or even easily. Sometimes bi and trans activists found themselves protesting against the very gay and lesbian activists/organizers they had previously protested with! One such example comes from the 1996 Creating Change conference, run by the National Gay and Lesbian task force in America. Bi activist Lorriane Hutchins explains in 'Identities and Place':

> Things came to a head at the 1996 conference when the number of discriminatory acts and remarks against bisexuals and transgender people reached such a peak that a Bi/Trans Action at the main plenary on Saturday morning was planned. Before the keynote speeches began, activists took to the stage recounting examples of biphobic and transphobic offenses committed against them during that weekend conference. They asked everyone in the room who identified as bi and/or transgender, and/or who was an ally, to stand up and be counted and to vow to confront biphobic and transphobic actions and attitudes in the future. Although the Bi/Trans Action was not included in the Gay and Lesbian Task Force press release following the conference, they did note that the first significant conversation between bisexual and transgender activists and members of the administration had occurred that weekend. (Hutchins 2019, p.42)

Another watershed moment came during the 1993 March on Washington for Lesbian, Gay and Bi Equal Rights and Liberation, when Lani Ka'ahumanu gave her now infamous, 'It ain't over til the bisexual speaks' speech, as the first openly bi speaker at a March on Washington event. She opened with these words, which I think sum up the struggle for bi visibility beautifully:

I am a token, and a symbol. Today there is no difference. I am the token out bisexual asked to speak, and I am a symbol of how powerful the bisexual pride movement is and how far we have come.

I came here in 1979 for the March on Washington for Lesbian and Gay Rights. I returned in 1987 for the March on Washington for Lesbian and Gay Rights. I stand here today on the stage of the 1993 March on Washington for Lesbian, Gay and Bisexual Equal Rights and Liberation. (Ka'ahumanu 1993)

Other changes were less dramatic, although required no less mental fortitude, effort, strength, and courage from the bi activists involved. In many cases it took years for organizations, groups, and events that no doubt had bi people in them from the beginning to change their names to reflect that work. And of course, not all have. For example, Australia's biggest Pride is still called 'Sydney Gay and Lesbian Mardi Gras', despite, of course, being for many more people than just lesbians and gay men.

By the 1990s, bi groups and events were sprouting up all over the world and suddenly people started noticing. Of course, mainstream society confused them noticing that bi organizations were now a thing with bisexuality having suddenly popped into existence. In 1995 *Newsweek* published a cover story about bisexuality with the incredulous headline 'Not gay. Not straight. A new sexual identity emerges' (1995 was also the year this particular bisexual emerged from the womb – I like to think the two are related). It includes a lot of hilarious gems as well as some actually insightful quotes and statistics, but I particularly like this paragraph:

After a brief vogue during the sexual revolution...it moved back underground in the 1980s, pushed by fears of AIDS and by gay identity politics. Nobody knows how many bisexuals there are in the country, or just how bisexuality should be defined. Its existence alone makes many people uncomfortable; it suggests that all sexual identity might be subject to change or expansion, and that we may not ever really be able to fulfill our partners or be fulfilled ourselves.

Pink on top

As a tribute to the bi movement's achievements and to help gain visibility and a sense community, activist Michael Page created the bisexual flag in 1998. Michael was inspired by the so-called 'bi-angles': blue and pink triangles, with a purple over-lay. The flag is a simple design of three stripes: pink, purple, and blue. The pink stripe represents same-gender attraction, the blue different-gender attraction, and the purple in the middle represents the two states coming together as bisexuality, in a ratio of 2.1.2. The pink stripe is always at the top. The flag was unveiled by Michael on the now-defunct bicafe.com, on the site's first anniversary. 'The key to understanding the symbolism in the Bi Pride Flag is to know that the purple pixels of color blend unnoticeably into both the pink and blue, just as in the "real world" where most bi people blend unnoticeably into both the gay/lesbian and straight communities,' Michael wrote in his announcement post (Baxter-Williams 2015).

Since then the flag has flourished all over the world as a rallying point, a symbol of hope and pride and community. It is free for everyone to use, and Michael specifically released it to the public without copyright or licence for that reason. 'We wanted to let the larger world know that we were here, we're proud, and we demanded respect,' Wendy Curry, then president of BiNet USA, told Biscuit in 2015. 'The flag, unlike our pins and even t-shirts, was something we could rally behind as we demanded equality. It gave us a sense of power and strength, something that was lacking before' (Baxter-Williams 2015).

In 2020, BiNet USA, the group responsible for bi-cafe.com, tried to claim that they had copyright of the flag, as Michael was a volunteer for them when he created it, and he was inspired by conversations with other volunteers. They planned on charging licensing fees for people and organizations to use the flag. This did not go down with the online bi community.

Michael Page also helped inspire Monica Helms, the creator of the trans flag. 'He and I were talking and he said, "You know, the trans community could use a flag", she told *Gay City News* in 2019 (Tracy 2019).

Since the '90s, the global bisexual community has been plugging away at our fight for visibility, for recognition, for equal rights and opportunities. Along the way there have been some huge wins, and some big losses. 'It was all about that, but also community-building. So signposting and trying to build the community, and also trying to make the community look as big as it is, because it appears so much smaller than it is,' Libby Baxter-Williams told me when I asked what issues the bi community was focusing on in the early 2000s, when she first stumbled into activism. She continues:

It was the idea that the community had lasted, had already existed for a long time. It felt old, but also was really full of quite young people in their early twenties. That doesn't really mesh, but that's how it was. It felt like it had been around forever, which it had, because I date it to the beginning of the '80s when BiCon first started. It felt so radical and so political just to be in a majority bi space.

In 2018, I worked with Libby and a group of other activists to get the first ever Bi Pride Float into the London Pride parade. At that point, Pride in London had been going for 47 years and had never had a bi float. The First Bi Pride Float initiative, as we so imaginatively named it, was in response to a cock up in 2017, when Pride in London forgot to have any bi groups even marching in the entire parade, and reacted pretty badly when activists pointed out that this wasn't okay. The float was an amazing experience and, in the years since, the now-defunct collective, the London Bi Pandas, have picked up the slack and organized another float in 2019's Pride in London. But this incident was an important reminder that the bi community still has to fight for our visibility and inclusion.

In September of 2019, the charity Bi Pride UK hosted the UK's first ever Bi Pride (as the name might suggest). I was lucky enough to be able to attend and speak on the community panel about bi+ organizing. It was an amazing experience to spend the day surrounded by my people and too just how numerous we are: within the first hour of opening the doors, there was a queue looping around the hall and down the street!

So bi people have always been around, even when they didn't have a label for their feelings or desires, even when they were erased from public life by heteronormativity, or even when they were made invisible within the fight for queer liberation. Now, the bi community is becoming more and more visible every day and finding new ways to connect and push back against the issues we face. Over the next few chapters, we'll explore what those issues are as well as what the bi community looks like now.

CHAPTER 7

What Is Biphobia?

Bi people experience both homophobia and biphobia. Homophobia is the prejudice and oppression of people based on their same-gender attraction, and biphobia is the prejudice and oppression of people based on their multi-gender attraction. Stonewall explains:

> The Bisexual Index defines biphobia as the fear or dislike of someone who identifies as bi; someone who has an emotional and/or sexual attraction to more than one gender. Biphobia is usually based on misconceptions of what bi people are like and how they behave in relationships. The Stonewall School Report 2017 found that more than a third (36 per cent) of 11 to 19-year-olds 'frequently' or 'often' hear negative comments about bi people (biphobic language), for example, that bi people are 'greedy' or 'just going through a phase'. (Stonewall 2018, p.6)

Biphobia can affect people in a range of ways, from hearing comments about being greedy or untrustworthy, to experiencing intimate partner or sexual violence, to even being less likely to be granted asylum or being more likely to be convicted of a crime. Unlike homophobia, which is targeted at queer people by straight people, bi people can experience biphobia from both gay and straight communities. This is known as double discrimination (see Chapter 4), which is a very important term for exploring why the bi community faces many of the issues we do. Activist and writer Shiri Eisner points out:

> Bisexuals often experience verbal violence within 'LGBT' communities when speaking out about bisexuality. For example, a recent study examining online discussions about bisexuality in an LGBT environment discovered that 55 percent of the comments contained some form (or evidence) of biphobia or monosexism, meaning it is far likelier to encounter biphobic comments than to encounter support for bisexual people. (Eisner 2013a, p.79)

As we've already explored the stereotypes that bi people face when it comes to dating and relationships (see Chapter 5), this chapter will focus more on the mechanisms of biphobia, from both outside and inside the LGBTQIA+ community, before looking at how biphobia affects the bi+ community in Chapter 9.

Monosexism is the term used in academia to discuss the systematic mechanism of biphobia. In order to understand how people are affected by biphobia, we first need to understand monosexism and why it's so prevalent. Again, Shiri Eisner explains:

> Monosexism, as I see it, refers to the structural privileging of monosexual identities and behaviours. So, monosexism refers, for example, to the belief that one can only be either straight or gay, that it is better to be monosexual than bisexual*, that only

monosexual identities are 'real', that monosexual issues are the only ones deserving of attention, etc. (Eisner 2013b)

The main driving factor of monosexism is heterosexism: the belief that heterosexuality is the only right, natural, or valid sexuality. Our heterosexist society invalidates and suppresses any kind of relationships other than between cisgender men and women, as well as any desire or behaviour outside of that supposed 'norm'. Suppressing and invalidating bisexual desires and behaviours is one element of that. Without the suppression of bi identities, it would be much harder for straight people to access straight privilege.

In our binarist system, heterosexuality is seen as both an attraction to 'the opposite sex' (because non-binary genders are also erased and invisibilized) as well as a lack of attraction to the same sex. As these two states are seen as being at odds with each other, proof of one is considered proof enough of the other. So, if someone is seen dating someone of the different gender, it is assumed that they are heterosexual and can access the privileges associated with heterosexuality. However, bi people in different-gender relationships don't necessarily have access to these privileges, which we'll discuss in a bit.

BI THE WAY

When I was 15 or 16, I was starting to figure out that maybe I was bi. I was also dating someone I thought I would be with forever (as 15- and 16-year-olds are wont to do), so the only way I knew how to explore this topic was, well, suggest threesomes (at some point in the far future as we were saving ourselves for marriage). I mean, boys like threesomes with other girls, right? Apparently, I was pretty transparent through my insistence on being 'okay' if that 'was something he wanted to do' because he ended up stopping me and telling me about how a girlfriend he had a few years ago was bi and really into his sister instead of him. He asked me if I was bi (which I denied) and told me if I was, he would love me less. I shoved myself back in the closet I had just barely started to open pretty quickly, and did not even consider the possibility of being bi until months after we broke up and I started to realize how trash that relationship actually had been.

Jackie M.

On the flip side of this, an absence of (proof of) attraction to the same gender is also seen as evidence of different-gender attraction. So someone who never (publicly) dates anyone of the same gender is seen as having an absence of attraction to that gender and therefore an attraction to the 'opposite gender'. This combination is the key component of heteronormativity and is how queer people are able to pass or be coercively passed if they are not open about or do not constantly reinforce their same-gender attraction. In this way as well, monosexism and bi erasure are the underpinnings of conversion therapy. This torture that queer people are subjected to relies on the concept that desiring one gender cancels out the desire for 'the other' (it also relies on the gender binary), and that diminishing same-gender desire will increase different-gender desire, assuming that these two things are different poles on a scale, with people's desires moving up and down the scale.

Bisexuality makes it harder for straight people to prove their heterosexuality because displaying attraction to 'the opposite sex' doesn't necessarily mean they aren't also attracted to 'the same sex', and therefore not actually heterosexual. So, in order to maintain access to heterosexual privilege, bisexuality needs to be suppressed and invalidated.

Although gay people are harmed by (and resist) heterosexism and heteronormativity, they are arguably collaborators in monosexism because bi identities make it harder to prove their homosexuality. This a threat because it can make it more complicated for gay people to organize around the shared oppression that same-gender attracted people face if there is no essence (remember the discussion we had about essentialism in Chapter 3? Here it is again) to that oppression.

Bisexuality also makes it harder to tell who the 'true gays' are because anyone attracted to the same gender might also be attracted to other genders, meaning it's more difficult to create an 'us vs them' narrative when fighting homophobia. Bisexuality also threatens what is called the 'immutability defence' when fighting against institutional homophobia. The 'immutability defence' is basically the 'born this way' argument. Bi+ people make it harder to argue that queer people 'can't help' their same-gender attraction and desire and therefore shouldn't face discrimination for it, because bisexuals are seen as being able to choose to just be or act straight, yet we refuse to. We'll see this argument come up again and again as we explore biphobia within the LGBTQIA+ community.

Professor Kenji Yoshino first put forward this theory of straight people benefiting from and gay people being complicit in monosexism in his essay 'The Epistemic Contract of Bisexual Erasure'. He sums it up as such:

> Bisexuality threatens all of these interests because it precludes both straights and gays from 'proving' that they are either straight or gay. This is because straights (for example) can only

prove that they are straight by adducing evidence of cross-sex desire. (They cannot adduce evidence of the absence of same-sex desire, as it is impossible to prove a negative.) But this means that straights can never definitively prove that they are straight in a world in which bisexuals exist, as the individual who adduces cross-sex desire could be either straight or bisexual, and there is no definitive way to arbitrate between those two possibilities. Bisexuality is thus threatening to all monosexuals because it makes it impossible to prove a monosexual identity. (Yoshino 2000, p.4)

The way in which bi+ identities are seen as a challenge to gay and lesbian attempts at forming communities and opposing heterosexism is best exemplified through the debates that happened within the lesbian communities in the '70s and '80s. Paula Rust, a feminist sociologist, gives probably the most in-depth exploration of this in her book *Bisexuality and the Challenge to Lesbian Politics*, in which she explains why lesbian feminists, in particular, have such overwhelming negative views of bisexual women. Paula suggests that it's because bi women threaten the feminist construction of lesbianism as the logical end-point of feminist ideals, as well as an inherently superior choice for women under the patriarchal oppression. She explains:

The construction of lesbianism as an essential characteristic made lesbian feminism vulnerable by creating the unfalsifiable possibility that there might also be a bisexual essence... If there is a bisexual essence, then many women who had been declared to be lesbians on the basis of their identity or behaviour might really be bisexuals. Consistent with their belief in the essentiality of lesbianism, lesbians would be morally compelled to recognize the bisexuality of these women to be as legitimate as their own lesbianism; in other words, it would compel them to acknowledge the 'loss' of a number of lesbians whose lesbian essence could no more be proved than their bisexual essence could be disproved. (Rust 1995, p.194)

From this quote, we can see that accepting the validity of bisexuality was seen as a threat to the lesbian community because it would mean acknowledging that many of their sisters and ancestors were in fact not lesbians. It would also undermine many of the arguments used by lesbian feminists to construct lesbianism as inherently more feminist and subversive to heterosexuality, because lesbianism 'denies men of their personal servants' (p.130), allows women to see the patriarchy unclouded by love for individual men and the privileges of heterosexuality, and is the only way for women to learn to love themselves and each other beyond male objectification. 'Bisexual attraction is even more troubling because it demonstrates that those who know the pleasure of lesbianism can still feel heterosexual desire, thus calling into question the obvious superiority of lesbianism,' further explains Paula (p.196).

Paula also argues that resistance to stable categorization isn't just a quirk of bisexuality's nature, it was intentionally baked into the foundation of the movement by its foremothers and fathers: 'In addition to celebrating the diversity of the bisexual community, many bisexuals feel that the concept of bisexuality itself should "embrace fluidity, subtle shading, ambiguity, wide variance, and flexibility in sexual experience and response"... Thus, bisexuality and bisexuals resist being co-opted into categorical thinking and in doing so, remain a challenge to dichotomous sexuality. Again, the diversity of the bisexual community that makes it difficult for bisexuals to agree on a definition of bisexuality, provides bisexuals with a political purpose and an ideological position' (Avery 1993, quoted in Rust 1995, p.375). So the early bi movement chose to focus on negative stereotypes and overgeneralizations about the bi community (i.e. 'bi people aren't all non-monogamous'), rather than trying to make assertions about what bisexuals *are* (i.e. 'all bi people are monogamous'). This tradition of the bi community is still very much alive today in the way in which we focus on celebrating what makes our community diverse, rather than trying to find things that universally bind us all together.

Bisexuals are a problem child, then. In the eyes of both the heterosexual institution and gay/lesbian political theorists, we saw what both posited as 'the only option', 'the moral imperative', 'the natural option' for love and attraction and went 'Naaah'. Unlike straight and gay people, we actually are able to experience loving and desiring any gender, and instead of finding one to be the real, true, natural, superior way of living, we decided they were all pretty nice. In existing, we unwittingly knocked down the house of cards of both heterosexists and paternalistic lesbian feminists. We were, and still are, seen as a threat to both.

BI THE WAY

The first person I ever dated was a woman. That was when I was either 15 or 16. After that I exclusively dated men for about 7 years (not intentionally it's just how it goes sometimes in a heteronormative society). In college I had become really good friends with a person who had come out as a lesbian our sophomore year. She knew I was pansexual and had been out since high school. We happened to both go through breakups at the same time and got even closer. Eventually, she kissed me. I coyly said I hadn't kissed a girl in 7 years and I forgot how great it was. After that, she wrote me a long note asking me if I wanted to be her girlfriend. I was still reeling from my breakup and she was still living with her ex, so I said I needed some time to think it over. She obliged and [a few weeks later] texted me and asked if we could talk. I said sure. I had made up my mind that we shouldn't date because I just wasn't in a place to give the affection she needed, but what she did was the nail in the coffin. When she showed up the first thing she did was hand me three books on 'the lesbian experience' and 'coming to terms with your identity' and said, 'I think these will help you.' I was astounded. I had been out and secure with my identity since I was 15. She had been out all of two years and just because she had a girlfriend more recently than I had and because she was a lesbian she thought she had the authority to educate me about being gay. I found out later that she had made other biphobic comments to some of my bi friends like 'I wouldn't date a bisexual because they're more likely to cheat.'

Luna Schäfer

This doesn't necessarily mean that monosexism is a particular problem in lesbian communities, more that the tradition of heated debate within lesbian and feminist subcultures makes it easier to find resources that exemplify how and why gay people as well as straight people can have a stake in it. But, it's important to note that gay monosexual people do not have the cultural power to oppress bi+ people in the way straight monosexuals do. As I've explained in a previous article about monosexism and biphobia (Shearing 2018c):

This doesn't mean that both gay and straight have the same systematic power over non-monosexuals. In fact, gay people have none. But their identity fitting into the binary structure of how sexuality is conceptualised in mainstream Western society means they have more visibility in society, and while that can exacerbate oppression, there's proof that this also comes with benefits that non-monosexuals don't have access to.

Because of this misconception, many people argue that 'monosexual' is an offensive word that lumps gay men/lesbians in with their oppressors by suggesting they both have the same amount of power as straight people to oppress bi people. But, this could be argued for all descriptors used to define groups of different powers and experiences. For example, 'woman' lumps straight and queer women together, as well as white women and women of colour, abled women and disabled women, etc. While descriptors like 'cis', 'straight', and 'monosexual' do erase the important differences between people in those groups, they are a vital tool for people outside of those labels to define and organize around issues. As bi+ activist Miles Joyner explains:

The terms are not designed to make those inside of the category feel comfortable, rather they allow the other group to critique various parts of the social systems they are a part of and affected by. All cisgender individuals benefit from the fact that they are cisgender, just as all straight individuals benefit from the fact that they are straight. Ignoring the benefits of being attracted to a single gender, in a society that punishes MGA individuals through exclusion, heightened violence, and erasure of identity, is ignoring the very real effects of that exclusion. (Joyner 2017)

Language and biphobia

Denying bi people language to define and explain our experiences is a very common type of biphobia, especially in LGBTQIA+ spaces. Often, people's discomfort with the word 'monosexism' or 'monosexual' is expressed through hateful comments or posts about bi people or even denying that the experiences of bi people are legitimate or our own. For example, it's common for people to claim that monosexism doesn't exist at all, or that biphobia is just a subtype of homophobia. It's not uncommon for bi girls to be told that we can't reclaim the slur 'dyke', even if we've been called it, claiming that the word 'dyke' is a slur against lesbians, and any time a bi woman is called a 'dyke' she is experiencing 'misdirected homophobia'. This claim makes me angry for a lot of reasons, but mostly because it's such a petty hill to die on. If a fellow queer woman tries to find power in a word that has been used to intimidate and threaten her and your response is to tell her she isn't the 'right kind of queer' – and that her experience with homophobia wasn't really even about her – you need to reconsider how much you care about your queer siblings. I've used the example of dyke here, but this also happens with bi men and non-binary people and other slurs.

BI THE WAY

The most prominent [biphobia I've experienced] lately has been getting dogpiled by people online whenever I talk about biphobia and honestly what helps me with that is hitting the books so to speak. Rather than looking towards randoms on Twitter and Tumblr and such for validation, I look towards the past and look at what we've actually been doing and have actually experienced. And I take my own experiences into account too and think 'these people are only saying these things because they think I don't experience this, or somehow think I experience it in a marginally different way' and find comfort and validation in that.

Kelli

Any bi person will tell you that homophobes do not care if we're not 'really gay'. People used to call me and my then-girlfriend 'dykes' back when we both identified solely as women, and she identified as a lesbian. They still called us dykes when we both identified as some flavour of genderqueer/non-binary and I still identify as bi. The people – usually men in my experience – who use that word to demean and intimidate us don't give a fuck about how we identify. They don't give a fuck about intra-community discourse. They see women who love women and who – in those moments of intimacy, at least – are forsaking men, and that makes us dykes in their eyes.

No one has ever apologized to someone they just called a dyke or a fag after learning they're actually bisexual, not gay. No one has ever stopped raping or beating someone for the same reason. Bi people do not get our hours reduced rather than being fired by homophobic employees. We are not offered to sleep on the streets only some nights by our unaccepting families.

To say that bi people cannot reclaim homophobic slurs is to deny our struggle against homophobia and heternormativity. It denies our community's history and ongoing role in LGBTQIA+ activism. Its only purpose is to push bisexuality out of our joint history and community with gay people in order to 'purify' both of those things. It's also rooted in biphobia. It's also rooted in the idea that bisexuality isn't real or valid enough of an identity to experience oppression, and therefore, we can only experience homophobia, not biphobia or monosexism. Denying bi people access to words to discuss our lives is a way of defining our lives out of existence because they don't fit the standard model of sexuality – aka monosexism.

As Orna Izkakson says in their essay 'If Half of You Dodges a Bullet, All of You First': 'It not my intention to accept our oppressors' definitions of our identity, but it is unrealistic – and conceivably life-threatening – to ignore the way they codify their bigotry' (p.251). If there are people willing to kill me or deny me my rights because my attraction to women makes me a dyke or a queer, then I am a dyke and a queer.

BI THE WAY

I came to terms with the fact that I was bi at about 15, and never had that much of an issue with it. A couple of my friends at the time were gay or queer, my boyfriend at the time didn't seem to have any issues with it, it was sort of a non-issue.

When I went to drama school I told people as and when it came up, but it never occurred to me that I needed to come out to new people. I met a man and we got together in my second year, and one night about a month in I made an offhand comment that made it clear I was not straight. I sort of tried to laugh it off apologizing that I had forgot to tell him, he seemed a bit weird but the conversation moved on. He was icy with me for a while, until one day it kind of exploded into a two-day 'fight' (on his part not mine). My memories of this fight are pretty hazy, I mainly just remember being completely terrified, but I think it went something like this:

1) by not telling him I was being deliberately deceitful and I wasn't the person he thought I was. 2) he was going to have to compete with women now too, and I was going to cheat on him with a woman. 3) this explained my preference for oral and my inability to cum from penetration. Was I imagining women as he went down on me? 4) had I ever slept with a woman? (I hadn't at this point.) Then I couldn't possibly be queer. 5) why would I say I was then? Why would I lie? 6) clearly I said it for attention as a teenager and it stuck. 7) he was willing to forgive me and stay with me despite this if it never came up again. 8) no one else would have someone that has this much of an issue with themselves and with the truth, so think about how lucky I am and how much it would wreck me to lose him.

I left that conversation feeling very grateful that he had stayed with me. This man was obsessed with the idea that he knew when you were lying, and so none of the above points was up for debate. This meant I also firmly left this conversation believing that I was heterosexual, that I was a pathological liar and an attention seeker, and my preferences in bed meant that there was something wrong with me.

Caitlin

As we explored a bit in Chapter 2, slurs aren't the only words that bi people aren't allowed to use, according to some: it's a common claim that bi women can't use the descriptors 'butch' or 'femme' as these are 'lesbian-specific words' and a way of describing gender expression 'free from male influence'. This is biphobic in that it denies bi women our place in the history of women who love women, especially as there was no meaningful difference between bi and lesbian communities and identities at the height of butch/femme culture, meaning women who might today identify as bi would have been part of the butch/femme scene. I also take umbrage at the idea that bi women's entire gender identity/expression revolves around men because some of us are sometimes attracted to them. This belief system seems to be left over from '70s-style lesbian separatism that bi women are tainted by men, or that we don't have an identity or autonomy beyond our relationship to men. This is a common thread of biphobia aimed at bi women from within the LGBT-QIA+ community.

'When people criticize me because I must be subconsciously centering or performing for men simply because I am attracted to them, it reeks of both misogyny and biphobia. It holds me to an impossible standard. And it sounds like when cishet men see women dressed up in public spaces and wonder aloud, "if women didn't want our attention, why would they look like that?"' writes activist and founder of Bi Girls Club, Gabrielle Alexa (n.d.).

When accusations are levelled against me or bi people in general that part of our attraction is a 'false consciousness', I am reminded of Julia Serano's comments about bisexuality being accused of upholding the gender binary (see Chapter 3). We must look at who is being accused of what and why. I can't know what my desire or gender expression would be like without patriarchal or heterosexist influence; no one can. But our identities, orientations, and the labels we use to describe these are the intersection of our inner worlds and the language we have created. The way everyone desires is unique and therefore uniquely influenced by the power structures we live in. The way I have experienced desire best fits with the term 'bisexual', so that it is the label I stuck with. Whether I would use something different if we lived in a different culture without patriarchy or the Western gender binary is something I can neither know nor make time to care about. There's too much organizing to do in this reality.

Of course, being accused of not really being attracted to one gender or another is not exclusive between bi women and lesbians. In fact, this is one of the most common types of biphobia. I don't think there is a single person who hasn't, or won't, be asked or told that they're not really attracted to certain genders. This type of biphobia is so pervasive that I recently had an ex-therapist subtly suggest that perhaps more young women are identifying as bi because of how sexualized women are in our culture; we confuse objectifying women through the male gaze as eroticizing them. I wasn't really sure what to say to that at the time, other than 'Hey, can we get back to talking about why I'm so depressed?'

Trying to deny or invalidate bi experiences and lives are forms of biphobia as well as bi erasure. Bi erasure is pretty much what it sounds like: the intentional or incidental erasure of bisexuality, bi experiences, lives, history, and community. We'll go into more depth about bi erasure and its impacts in the bi community in the next chapter.

The pillars of biphobia

Like homophobia and transphobia, biphobia rears its ugly head in a multitude of ways, both interpersonally and systematically. Systematically, biphobia would be the barriers facing bi people when attempting to access things like healthcare, legal services, education, work, etc. In Chapter 9, 'What Issues Do Bi People Face', we'll dive into how biphobia impacts our community as a whole. Interpersonal biphobia consists of verbal harassment, micro-aggressions, exclusion, and violence, particularly sexual and intimate partner violence.

BI THE WAY

I'm 21 and I'm currently out to most of my friends, but not my family. That's all on hold because I'm not sure my father will react well if I tell him, and I still live with my parents. It bothers me because it doesn't feel like I can be fully myself at home.

When it comes to coming out, most of my friends were understanding and they didn't react in a homophobic or biphobic way. That wasn't the case when I came out to some uni friends. They were very accepting and kind, but one of them asked me in all seriousness if my bisexuality was going to evolve into lesbianism. (I said, 'Absolutely not.') I've had my fair share of therapists, and while one of them was totally fine when I came out to her, the first one I came out to was, again, accepting and kind, but then said I would one day have to choose to date a person of a specific gender – implying that I would have to pick a side. I also once told my mom when I was questioning my sexuality that I knew I liked boys but I wasn't sure about girls, so I might be bisexual. She said she would still accept and support me if I decided to date a girl 'and become a lesbian'.

Anonymous

Both systematic and interpersonal biphobia stem from the same (or at least similar) prejudices, stereotypes, and misconceptions about bi people, the most common of which are:

- **Bi people are untrustworthy** – this misconception is linked to the belief that bisexuality isn't a real identity and therefore anyone who says they're bi must be lying. If someone is lying about who they are, surely they're going to lie about other things, right? Systematically, this prejudice makes it harder for bi people to be believed in legal situations, particularly in asylum cases. Interpersonally, bi people are often treated with suspicion in relationships, being considered more likely to cheat or generally be deceptive. This has a direct impact on the rates of intimate partner violence experienced by bi people, especially bi women, as this distrust can translate into jealousy and controlling behaviour. Other ways it can manifest interpersonally would be people refusing to date bi people because 'they always cheat' or 'can't be trusted'. Klein sums up this suspicion:

  > The bisexual resembles the spy in that he or she moves psychosexually freely among men and among women. The bisexual also resembles the traitor in that he or she is in a position to know the secrets of both camps, and to play one against the other. The bisexual, in short, is seen as a dangerous person, not to be trusted, because his or her party loyalty, so to speak, is nonexistent. And if one lacks this sort of loyalty, one is so far outside the human sexual pale that one is virtually nonexistent. (Klein [1978] 2014, p.7)

- **Bi people are unstable** – similar to the idea that bi people are untrustworthy, this biphobic stereotype stems from the perception that bi identities are less valid or whole than gay or straight identities and are therefore less stable. This is also linked to the monosexist belief that bi identities are 'stopovers' on the way to realizing your 'full' sexuality. So, because bisexuality is seen as unstable, bi people are as well. We are considered flaky, confused, unable to commit to one gender and therefore unable to commit in general, and even mentally unstable. In her research, Paula Rust found several lesbians responded that bi women are mentally unstable when asked what they thought about bi women. 'It does not exist. To be bisexual would mean that a person were simultaneously involved in an intimate sexual relationship with a man and a woman. It is possible but would be better described as a schizophrenic,' wrote one respondent (p.91). In a similar study by French sociologist Daniel Welzer-Lang exploring gay men and lesbians' feelings towards bi people, 4.5 per cent linked bisexuality to 'psychological suffering' in their answers. 'Choice distresses them,' replied one participant. This type of biphobia mostly materializes in people's lives as disparaging comments or comments invalidating bi people's identities, but it can also have an effect on bi people's ability to be believed or taken seriously when trying to access healthcare (particularly mental healthcare), asylum, or legal services.

- **Bi people are hypersexual** – this specific biphobic prejudice has one of the most profound effects on the bi community because it is a factor in the extremely high rates of sexual violence we face. The 'logic' behind this faux maxim is that a person is only bi because they are too insatiable to be satisfied by just one gender and therefore they turn to other genders in order to have access to more potential partners. Because of this, bi people are seen as greedy, 'always up for it', unable to be monogamous, more likely to cheat, and only interested in sex. It is also the root of a lot of biphobic fetishization, especially when it comes to bi women, as bi people are seen as more sexually liberal, kinky, and even exotic. That last one is especially an issue for bi women of colour, who are seen as exotic already because of their ethnicity. For bi men, being seen as hypersexual is very closely linked to the next stereotype that bi people spread sexual diseases.

- **Bi people are a vector of disease** – since the AIDS crisis in the '80s, bi people, particularly bi men, have been seen as responsible for spreading sexually transmitted diseases between gay and straight people. As AIDS and HIV were originally seen as diseases that only affected gay men, bi people were considered one of the key ways that they spread from gay men to straight people and gay women. During the crisis, and for a long time after (even to this day, in some places), bi men were seen as deviants who would carry the infection to their unsuspecting wives and girlfriends after having illicit affairs with men. 'In the minds of many heterosexual Americans, bisexuality has come to be strongly identified with images of married, dishonest, closeted men sneaking out on their unsuspecting wives, contracting AIDS through unsafe sex with other men, then infecting their innocent wives and children,' writes Yoshino in 'The Epistemic Contract of Bisexual Erasure' (2000, p.34). Bi women who slept with men were also seen as the only possible bridge for AIDS to cross from queer men into lesbian communities. When asked about whether they were worried about the risk of HIV, 14 respondents in Crust's survey mentioned bi women as a specific risk to lesbians. No other group was mentioned as being seen as a risk.

It's hard to overestimate the effect that the AIDS crisis had on the bi community. As the crisis worsened and spread from mostly affecting queer people and drug users – who were seen as expendable – to 'the general public' (aka straight people), bisexuals, especially bi men, were used as scapegoats. In being blamed for the spread, this was the first time that bisexuality was ever discussed in mainstream media, when its assumed connection to AIDS was splashed across front pages. In a way, bisexuality entered mainstream public consciousness as a spectre of the AIDS crisis ('AIDS Specter for Women: The Bisexual Man' decried one headline in The New York Times in 1987; Nordheimer 1987), and the two remained linked in many people's minds for decades to come. The crisis also stalled the momentum of the early bi movement that emerged in the '70s for several reasons. First, many bi activists died of AIDS-related illness, as we saw in Chapter 6 on bi history. Other activists decided to focus their efforts on general HIV/AIDS activism rather than specifically bi activism, including one of the founders of The Bisexual Center. Many bi people chose to stay closeted or re-closet themselves in order to avoid stigma, which as well as having an impact on the people themselves, stymied the bi communities' push for visibility and movement building.

If, like me, you entered this world in the decades after the AIDS crisis, I strongly recommend that you take the time to learn about it. I don't think it's possible to understand queer experiences, community, and queerphobia without it. We lost a generation of queer men (and many queer women and non-binary people) in a matter of years, and that loss and the impact on our community can still be felt today. On top of that, bi and trans people (as well as sex workers and drug users) are often erased from the narrative around the AIDS crisis, but our bi and trans ancestors fought and died too, and we cannot let the memory of them disappear.

- **Bi people are traitors** – this stereotype comes almost exclusively from members of the gay and lesbian community who see bi people as traitors to the cause of gay liberation. 'I believe now, that if bisexual women had an ounce of sexual politics, they would stop sleeping with men,' prominent transphobe Julie Bindel wrote as recently as 2012 (Bindel 2012). As we've seen in Chapter 6 about bi history, it definitely isn't the case that bi people deserted the queer cause. This suspicion of the bi community has led some gay men and lesbians to eschew bi people as friends, partners, and comrades. This type of biphobia also overlaps with the idea that bi women are traitors to feminism or 'sleeping with the enemy' if we choose to have relationships with men.

- **Bi women are tainted by men** – similar to the previous example, this type of biphobia mainly comes from lesbians, directed at bi women, although it is rooted in misogynistic 'virginity culture' and the notion that penetrative sex changes a woman. This manifests in bi women's lives as verbal harassment, negative comments, and refusal to date bi women. One particularly nasty example I've heard is a lesbian telling a bi woman she could 'smell the cum on her' breath after she came out as bi to her. Another example comes from the now infamous

Arielle Scarcella's now infamous video, 'What Lesbians Think About Bisexuals' (2013), which as the name suggests, includes lesbians talking about what they think of bi women. None of their thoughts are particularly flattering and of course don't represent lesbians as a whole. One of the video's participants graciously says that if a bi woman is funny and attractive enough, she can overlook 'the fact that [you] had a dick in [your] mouth last week'.

This video had a huge effect on my coming out when I stumbled across it as a young teen, and it made me feel like I wouldn't be welcome in the queer community or ever be attractive to other women because I also liked men. But since watching that video, I've long since stopped caring about what lesbians think of my bisexuality. Don't get me wrong, I care about what individual lesbians think of me as a person. Do they like me? Would they call on me as a community organizer and activist? Do they think I'm a good person? And most importantly, after a few glasses of wine, do they think I'm cute? But what they as a capital L Lesbian think of my capital B Bisexuality? I just don't give a shit. In fact, it's got to the point that if anyone (who isn't bi) tries to tell me 'what they think of bisexuality' I find a way to excuse myself or ignore it, because it rarely ends well, and as I cross the hump of my mid-20s, I'm finally learning to value my time and headspace. For me, it comes down to these simple facts: bisexuality is real. Bi people have been part of the struggle for sexual equality since the beginning. Bi people's experiences and issues deserve space and attention. What anyone thinks of that beyond 'how can we work together to achieve our collective liberation?' is no concern of mine. Our existence has been debated too much for too long for any other stance to be possible. I wish the energy upon you, too, dearest reader.

BI THE WAY

When I came out to a group of friends, one of them who is a cis man said, 'I totally support you, but I hope you don't "turn" my wife.' At the time, I just laughed it off (I was a little drunk, to be honest) but when I thought about it later, it bugged me. Does he really think I have the power to turn people bisexual? I only wish I could have this superpower.

Anonymous

Intersectionality and biphobia

Biphobia isn't one size fits all, and it affects different demographics of bi people in different ways. For example, black bi people are more likely to be seen as hypersexual, as sexual aggressiveness and hypersexuality are racist stereotypes applied to black people, dating back to slavery and colonialism. On the flip side of this, disabled bi people may find their orientation being erased, as disabled people are often seen as uninterested in or incapable of sexual or romantic relationships. 'I have encountered a double stigma when mentioning my bisexuality – there is of course, a stereotype that bisexuals are greedy and noncommittal. People have extended that perception towards me by saying that being greedy won't make dating with a disability easier,' explained my friend Grace. '[That] kind of attitude...perpetuates a dangerous, completely inaccurate idea that disabled people are desperate and should feel lucky for any attention we get.' Trans bi people may be more likely to be considered unstable, compounding the transphobic notion that trans people are confused about their gender or mentally unwell. More research into how biphobia intersects with other discrimination and the impacts this has is desperately needed. As a whole, the bi movement could also stand to provide more space for bi people who experience multiple types of oppression to share and explore their experiences and to receive relevant and adequate support.

How common is biphobia?

Biphobia is incredibly pervasive. Studies have shown that bi people are less accepted than gay men and lesbians. For example, in one study conducted in 2001 at San Francisco State University, 53 per cent of participants said they found gay men and lesbians 'acceptable', compared to 46 per cent who said the same about bi men and women (Herek 2002). A similar study from Indiana University Bloomington in 2016 found that changing attitudes towards bisexuality was lagging behind those for lesbians and gay men, having only moved from 'negative to neutral' (Dodge et al. 2016). Bi men lagged behind bi women in terms of perceived acceptability, although it's important to remember that what's seen as acceptance for bi women is often just fetishization from straight men.

In 2017, Stonewall found that 35 per cent of 11- to 19-year-olds had 'frequently' or 'often' heard biphobic comments (Bradlow 2017). On top of that, one in three bi teens have experienced bullying because of their sexuality, are less likely than their gay/lesbian peers to be able to talk at home about their sexuality, and are more likely to self-harm. Teens who identify as pan or queer were even more likely to have self-harmed: 79 per cent of pan/queer teens compared to 67 per cent of bi teens.

As Bowling for Soup warns us, the things that plague us in

school don't always end when we graduate. A study conducted by *William & Mary Journal of Women and the Law* in 2015 found that one in three bi people have heard biphobic jokes at work (Tweedy and Yescavage 2015), while in a report by the Equality Network here in the UK from the same year, half of bi respondents reported experiencing biphobia when accessing healthcare (Rankin, Morton, and Bell 2015).

So if biphobia is so common, why does it seem to go so unnoticed, with so many people still claiming that bi people 'get the best of both worlds' or even have 'bi privilege'? In the next chapter, we'll explore how bi lives and experiences are denied or ignored because of bi erasure, before moving on to look at the impacts biphobia and bi erasure have on our community overall.

CHAPTER 8

What Is Bi Erasure?

As I mentioned in Chapter 4, bi erasure is pretty much what it sounds like: the intentional or incidental erasure of bisexuality, bi experiences, lives, history, and community. Stonewall describes it as:

> Bi erasure is a form of biphobia where the legitimacy or existence of being bi as a sexual orientation is questioned or denied, often based on an assumption that there are only two forms of sexual orientation – straight and gay. Bi erasure is not always malicious and is often due to the lack of bi-visibility in everyday life. (Stonewall 2018, p.8)

As you might have guessed from the name of Kenji Yoshino's essay on monosexism, 'The Epistemic Contract of Bi Erasure' (2000), bi erasure is the key way in which monosexism is upheld. Like biphobia, bi erasure happens on both structural and interpersonal levels. An example of structural bi erasure is the lack of adequate health care for bisexual people because it is assumed that our issues will be covered by healthcare targeted at gay or straight people. On an interpersonal level, bi erasure might look like friends or loved ones calling you gay or straight, depending on your current or most recent relationship.

Bi erasure is so pervasive that even discussions and examples of bi erasure are invalidated or go unreported. The claim that bi people have a unique privilege within the LGBTQIA+ community because it is assumed that all of us have the ability to have 'straight' or at least 'straight-passing' relationships relies on different types of bi erasure. The first is the erasure of non-binary and gender non-conforming bi people, whose relationships may never look 'straight', and assuming they are in a different-gender relationship may be misgendering them. Second, it ignores the realities facing the bi community, such as experiencing higher rates of sexual and domestic violence, higher rates of mental illness, worse physical health outcomes, increased likelihood of living in poverty, higher rates of addiction, and several other issues, which we will cover in the next chapter.

BI THE WAY

I'm AFAB (announced female at birth) non-binary and I came out as bi at 15. I very rarely felt attraction to anyone but started having feelings for and started dating my friend. Although I identified as bi the narrative that bisexuality is a phase/bridge for coming out as gay at the time was persistent, and consistently being told I was a lesbian along with the fact I rarely felt attraction anyway meant that I assumed they were right. Although I was out to some close friends and my family, I was not out at school and after doing one year of sixth form at the same school I decided to transfer to a different college for my second year. When I moved I decided to be fully out for the first time and introduced myself as gay, my girlfriend and I broke up a couple of months later and shortly after I ended up in a relationship with a guy. The misinformation/narrative about bisexuality was enough for me to come out as gay because I was convinced I could not be bi.

Rowan

I have found the term 'relative benefits' much more useful than 'privilege' when discussing intra-community experiences. Having privilege means having access to unearned benefits because of who you are. For example, I experience a lot of unearned benefits because of my whiteness, including being more likely to get a job than a candidate of colour with the same experience, being less likely to be murdered by the police, and being less likely to go to prison. I don't have to hide any parts of myself or be perceived as something I'm not. They are not situational; I always have access to white privilege.

On the other hand, I only experience the privileges of being perceived as able-bodied in certain situations, because of my invisible illness. When I'm just walking down the street, I don't receive the kinds of harassment that people who use wheelchairs or canes do, but in other situations such as accessing medical care or when I'm using my inhaler in public, I am forced to navigate ableist stigma.

When a bi man turns up to an office party with his girlfriend, he has access to the relative benefits of not being asked invasive questions about his sex life, but this comes at the cost of being coercively passed. When I'm welcomed into a supportive group of queers because I've proved myself by having a girlfriend, the relative benefits of not facing double discrimination often come at the price of playing down my attraction to men. I have been in both these situations, and knowing I would not be welcome if I were fully out/with some else has a big impact on my mental wellbeing.

As we've seen (and will explore more in the next chapter), gay men and lesbians have access to lots of relative benefits that bi people don't, such as better community support, better access to mental healthcare that caters to their real self, being less like to live in poverty or experience sexual violence than bi people, etc. On the other hand, many bi people have the relative benefits of being less likely to experience street homophobia, or having genuine relationships without having to come out to their family, for example. But all of these things are situational and rely on a level of closeting or erasure.

BI THE WAY

I was pissed off because my sister's then-boyfriend (now fiancé) was in a fight with their roommate about whether or not bi people experience homophobia (roommate who is bi said yes, sister's bf who is straight and trans said no), and I was complaining about it to my mom. My mom said, 'Well maybe [sister's fiancé] feels strongly about it because it's, like, closer to his own experience' and I said 'Mom it's *my* experience' and she was like 'oh' like she had clearly forgotten I'm bi.

Olivia

They are also very dependent on other intersections of bi people's identity, including gender. If I were to walk down the street wearing a T-shirt that says 'I'm bisexual' with a man, I most likely wouldn't face any harassment, because I'd be seen as being 'protected by' or even belonging to that man, even if we weren't a couple. On that other hand, a man wearing the same shirt with a woman might experience harassment, because he wouldn't be seen as 'manly enough' to defend himself or deserving of the woman he was with. But, if we were to repeat the experiment walking alone, the bi woman is much more likely to experience harassment, especially catcalling. So the idea behind 'passing privilege' makes a lot of assumptions about gender and gender conformity, as well as erasing bi people's identities.

Again, we could also question here who is being accused of having privilege or upholding the status quo, and why. Femme queer women often have their identity erased and invalidated, but the concept of 'femme privilege' is much less pervasive than the concept of 'bi privilege'. In my experience, trying to classify who has privilege over whom in our community is nothing but counterproductive and exhausting and inevitably ends in hurt on all sides.

Erasure of biphobia

Bi erasure is often the focus of the bi movement's efforts, as it is seen as the root of many of the key issues in the bi community. This is sometimes confused with campaigning for visibility for visibility's sake, because even the violence committed against the bi community and the issues caused by erasure are not measured. For example, in 2019 two women out on a date in London were left beaten and bloodied after they refused to kiss in front of a group of teenage boys. All the media coverage at the time described it as an attack on a 'lesbian couple', with many public figures (rightfully) calling out the danger of violence against lesbians. However, one of the women is actually bisexual and was met with some backlash, especially by some of the UK's transphobic hate groups, after using the attack as an opportunity to highlight the violence against the most marginalized members of the queer community, especially queer people of colour and trans people.

> **BI THE WAY**
>
> When I first attended [a large international LGBTQIA+ conference], I was hoping I would be welcomed as an LGBT activist. I was referred to loudly, again and again as 'that straight bloke from Stonewall'. I was running a session on bi erasure, I was in the profile. Also, there were straight people there that weren't called 'that straight guy'. It was said to insult me.
>
> *Dominic Arnall*

In another example, in 'The Hate Crime Report: Homophobia, Biphobia and Transphobia in London' done by Galop in 2013 (which seems to be the most recent report despite already being eight years old), no data was recorded about bi people's experiences with biphobic prejudice or violence. They addressed this by saying:

> At present the police record whether a crime was motivated by sexual orientation hatred. Theoretically, that label could include homophobia, biphobia and anti-heterosexual hatred. Practically it is always used to describe homophobic crime. Therefore, there is no data on biphobia. (Antjoule 2013)

After learning that the Metropolitan Police track all sexuality- or gender identity-motivated hate crime as either homo- or trans-phobic, I submitted a Freedom of Information (FOI) request to both the Met and the National Police Chiefs' Council (NPCC) (if you've never submitted an FOI request, I highly recommend trying it; it's a great way to get information and to remind public bodies that they owe us transparency), requesting to see how many hate crimes they had recorded as being motivated by biphobia. Both confirmed that there was not aggregated data available, although the NPCC suggested that regional LGBT liaison officers might hold that information. This means that biphobic violence and hate crimes have been erased within reporting and we don't have a view of how widespread bipho-bic violence is in the UK. This doesn't mean I think we as a community should put any focus on working with police or expecting them to protect us or arbitrate our experiences. This is just another example of the ways in which bisexual people are left without services that others have access to.

It also wasn't until 2015 that 'biphobia' was recognized as part of International Day Against Homophobia, Biphobia, Intersex-ism and Transphobia (now often referred to as 'IDAHOBIT'). Even in 2017, Stonewall only mentions bisexual twice and biphobia 11 times in their report into hate crime and discrimination in the UK (Bachmann and Gooch 2017). Because of this lack of reporting, we don't have a picture of how frequently and to what extent the bi community experiences biphobic hate crimes.

Bi erasure in the media

But it's not just biphobia that goes unrecognized because of bi erasure; all aspects of the bi experience, community, lives, and identities are invisibilized and even invalidated. Bisexuality and bi issues often go under-reported and under-represented in both news and entertainment media. For example, in the last 12 months, the word 'bisexual' has only appeared in the UK mainstream news outlets 1627 times, compared to 'gay' 14,412 times, 'lesbian' 3278 times, and 'trans'/'transgender' a total of 9170 times. The vast majority of the mentions of bisexuality were what I call 'and-bisexuals'; that is, they were not mentioned for their own sake, only alongside 'gay' or 'lesbian', as in 'gay and bisexual' (I conducted this very crude study in May 2020, using the LexisNexis library). I also found that in the same time frame, biphobia was only mentioned 70 times, compared to 1719 mentions of homophobia and 446 mentions of transphobia.

And it's not just mainstream media that either erases bisexuality or treats it as an afterthought. In an even cruder investigation, I found that in the last six months (again, starting from May 2020) PinkNews, Britain's leading LGBTQIA+ news website, only mentioned the word 'bisexual' or openly bi people in 22 headlines and 'pansexual' only 8 times, out of the hundreds of articles they published in that time frame.

> **BI THE WAY**
>
> My husband came out as bi and said 'as a straight woman this must be hard for you to understand' and...he'd forgotten I was bi. He's aware of the (barely) relationships I had with women as a late teen. So he 'knew', and was identifying himself as bi after a long personal struggle, but still conceived of me as straight.
>
> Ashley

Another historic and somewhat ironic example of bi erasure

comes from the Gay Liberation Front in the UK in 1971. After the publication of the book *Everything You Ever Wanted to Know about Sex* (*But Were Afraid to Ask)* by Dr David Reuben, the group organized a letter-writing campaign to combat the homophobic and sexist stereotypes it contained. Several bi members of the group wrote criticism that pointed out the bi erasure in the book. However, these criticisms were themselves erased. 'By the publication of the final letter, however, which had 158 signatures, both of the points referencing bisexuality had been removed,' writes Martha Robinson Rhodes in the essay 'Bisexuality, Multiple-Gender-Attraction, and Gay Liberation Politics in the 1970s' (2020), which explores how bi+ identities were erased by early gay groups in the UK. The essay concludes: 'frequently, however, gay liberationists simply opted not to discuss bisexuality and multiple-gender-attraction at all. As in the final draft of the letter against Reuben, references to them were literally erased.'

While I was writing this chapter, the LGBT Foundation released statistics showing that during the 2020 Covid-19 lockdown, calls to the charity regarding biphobia increased 450 per cent (LGBT Foundation 2020). This shocking statistic was not reported by any of the mainstream media here in the UK. Yet again, the experiences of bi people were erased from mainstream consciousness and the danger bi+ people face was only recognized within our own community, contributing to the notion that bi people face less prejudice than the gay and lesbian community.

As well as under-reporting the experiences of and issues facing the bi community, the media often erases the bisexuality of celebrities and public figures. For example, Kristen Stewart is often called a gay or lesbian icon; while she is an icon, she identifies as bi (and is therefore a bicon). 'It's not confusing if you're bisexual. For me, it's the opposite,' KStew told the *Guardian* in 2017 (Brooks 2017). Lady Gaga is often described as an LGBTQIA+

'ally', despite coming out as bi early in her career. Tom Daley is an oft-cited example of how bisexuality is erased, even when people are trying to come out. Daley originally posted a YouTube video in 2013 revealing that he was in a relationship with a man and is attracted to men and women. PinkNews reported this as him coming out as gay.

As we've seen in earlier chapters, bisexuality is often completely erased within entertainment media. Stories are one of the most important ways in which people come to understand themselves and empathize with others. This isn't possible when certain types of people and experiences are absent in the majority of stories. GLAAD's 'Where We Are on TV' report, which has been running annually since 1995, has found there to be fewer bi characters and storylines than gay and lesbian characters and storylines. 'Bisexual+ characters make up 26% of all LGBTQ characters across all three platforms. This is a one percent decrease from last year, and far from the reality that bisexual+ people make up the majority of the community,' notes GLAAD in their most recent report (2019).

Bi erasure in entertainment media doesn't stop at there being fewer identifiable bi characters (although that would be bad enough). Often programmes and films have multi-gender attracted characters, yet still manage to erase their bi or pansexuality. In many cases, bi+ characters are written off as confused or unstable, or 'pick a side' by realizing that they were either straight or gay all along, depending on the gender of the partner they end up with (cough, Willow from *Buffy*, cough). In other cases, behaviourally bi characters will refuse to identify themselves, saying they don't like labels or that they 'just like people' (cough, Piper from *Orange Is the New Black*, cough) or their sexuality is played off as a joke (cough, Elliot/The Todd from *Scrubs*, cough).

BI THE WAY

I have experienced bi erasure in the workplace. About two years ago, I worked as a receptionist for a Massage Envy. Sometimes I would work nights. The owner's daughter worked as the main manager for our location. She identified as lesbian and for some reason, the topic of sexuality came up in conversation. Since I knew she was a part of the LGBTQIA+ community, I thought I was safe coming out as bisexual to her and the other manager. The two were long-time friends and the other manager was a cis-straight woman. They both proceeded to tell me that they don't think bisexuality exists. The owner's daughter proceeded to tell me of an experience she had with an ex-girlfriend where the girlfriend cheated on her with a man. She said the idea of being with a woman that has been with a man was absolutely disgusting to her. This all led me to believe she had a lot of trauma and a horrible experience with one person who identified as bisexual and lumped all other bisexual women as disgusting or nonexistent. It made me feel incredibly uncomfortable and I eventually left the job.

Lindsay

It's not possible to explore bi erasure in the media without looking at the role the male gaze plays. As Shiri Eisner points out in the chapter 'Bisexuality and Women' in *Notes for a Bisexual Revolution* (2013a), bi women are often presented in a way that caters to the male fantasy, while reassuring men that bi women are still more interested in them than women. Shiri, and others, have suggested that this also explains why there is such a lack of bi men represented in the media; they don't appeal to the cliched male fantasy of two girls and one guy. I explain this further in one of my first articles about bisexuality, called 'The Bisexual Erasure/Over-Sexualisation Feedback Loop' (I had not yet mastered the art of catchy titles):

> Acknowledging that a woman is really bisexual means acknowledging that she's not just doing it for men's attention, pleasure, and sexual fantasy. It means acknowledging that there is something about her sexuality that isn't for men, and accepting that a woman might decide to be with another woman and not a man.
>
> This idea of choice may also go some way to explaining why men's bisexuality is considered so taboo. Not only does male bisexuality play less of a role in the conventional male fantasy, it's harder to 'other' a man who has sex with/loves men if he also has sex with/loves women.

Academic bi erasure

'The New York Psychoanalytical Institute, one of the major organizations of its kind in America, and indeed, in the world, has in its library catalogue 600 items on the subject of homosexuality – and only 60 on bisexuality,' wrote Klein in his seminal book *The Bisexual Option*, which was published in 1978 (Klein [1978] 2014, p.3), and little has changed since then. As an experiment, I searched for 'homosexuality' in the British Library's archives, which returned 12,591 results, and 'bisexuality', which only returned 1986.

In order to maintain the status quo of the hetero/homo binary, bi identities have been erased from academic discourse, including queer theory. Professor Dawne Moon writes in her article 'How Queerness Erased Bisexuality':

Queer theorists spoke of disrupting binaries such as male/female and hetero/homo, but the fact that bisexuals' lived experience of gender disrupts both of those binaries never seemed to even enter the conversation. Even Judith Butler's 1993 *Bodies That Matter*, a book that was crucial in the development of queer theory, of the creation of new ways of being gendered, and of my own thinking, mentioned bisexuality only once – in a sentence expressing almost surprise that the term was being claimed by 'bisexuals and straights for whom the term expresses an affiliation with anti-homophobic politics' (p. 230). (Butler 1993, quoted in Moon 2016)

Steven Angelides writes that 'a particular temporal framing of sexuality has cast bisexuality in the past or future but never *in the present tense*' (Angelides 2001, p.17). Bisexuality is either seen as a futuristic state with no genders and labels, or it's seen as something binary and regressive. Never does it exist for its own sake. The misconception that 'everyone is bisexual' often relies on the idea that in a perfect world where there are no gender roles (or gender), heteronormativity, homophobia, or sexism, everyone might be attracted to any other person, making them what we currently call bi or pan. This claim is often used to diminish and erase bi people's experiences in two ways. First is outrightly denying that anyone can or should be bi in our current culture. The second is more subtle: if everyone is or has the capacity to be bisexual, then there's no reason for people to identify as bisexual and no need for bi people to have specific spaces or reasons.

Another reason why bi+ identities have been overlooked in queer theory is because they often evade a solid definition. As we saw in Chapter 6 about history, focusing more on what bisexuality isn't and leaving plenty of ambiguity and open space for what's included under the bi umbrella was an intentional move by the founders of the bi movement. This has made it difficult to use and write about as a fixed identity, starting point, or political position. 'However, queer theorization often relies on dichotomies when deconstructing these normativities, leaving bisexuality to be theorized as an absence, a middle group dependent solely on heterosexuality and homosexuality for its existence, and a cultural and political null,' write Voss, Browne, and Gupta (2014, p.1607). What that basically means is that queer theory often focuses on how one identity subverts or destabilizes another (usually gay identities in contrast to straight ones), leaving little room for how identities that contain elements of both and neither interact with these binaries. This is all getting pretty theoretical for a book that is intended to provide you with practical insight, but if you're interested in bi theory, I hope by now you can see that there is definitely a gap that needs to be filled. Get reading, get writing, and reach out to bi academics; I guarantee those nerds (of which I'm one) will be excited to talk to and help you.

The effects of bi erasure

So why does bi erasure matter? As we've seen, it makes it harder for bi people to understand themselves and find their community. It also means there are less protection, support, and services available specifically for bi people. 'In many parts of the UK there are a lack of local bisexual groups and events because bisexual specific work receives very little funding or mainstream support. This was the main difficulty identified by the 85% of respondents who only feel "a little" or "not at all" part of a bisexual community,' write Sam Rankin, James Morton, and Matthew Bell, in the report 'Complicated? Bisexual People's Experiences of and Ideas for Improving Services' (2015).

BI THE WAY

My friends now affectionately refer to the incident as 'Bi-gate' but at the time it was so embarrassing... My coursemates and I were sitting around a circle of desks during a seminar and we got to talking about people we found attractive, standard conversation really, and I talked about both men and women I liked. That obviously led to the usual round of questions – have you ever dated a woman, when did you first realize, who was your first crush, does that mean you fancy me, all the questions I'd been answering since I first came out at 15, so I wasn't mad. That was, until the girl sitting next to me (I'm not sure whether to name her), comes out with: 'Oh! I used to be bi too!' As politely and calmly as I could muster, I replied with, 'Oh right, what do you mean used to?'

She then followed the thought with: 'Well, when I was 15 I assumed I was bi because I thought women were attractive, but I would never, EVER date a woman and the thought of having sex with one completely disgusts me.' I'm used to having people say strange things when I first come out as bi to them, because I wouldn't say I was particularly out-there about it, but that was honestly the worst thing I've ever heard. In that moment, having just exposed something about myself to yet another group of people I hardly knew at the time, I felt that she had completely and utterly denounced the fact that people could be bi.

Molly

Bi erasure in law

One notable example of the effects of bi erasure is the way in which bi+ identities are often erased from legal protections due to the language used, despite bi people experiencing regular discrimination because of their bisexuality (not because of our proximity to gay identities, as some people have argued). The San Francisco Human Rights Commission (n.d., p.5) points out in its report 'Bisexual Invisibility: Impacts and Recommendations':

> In California, the chapter of the Christian Legal Society at Hastings College of the Law sued the school for not recognizing them as a registered student organization because they discriminate based on sexual orientation. The language of their petition uses orientation-neutral language, including identifying Hastings OUTLAW as 'a group advocating for the interests of homosexual and bisexual students'. Meanwhile, the law school's petition defending the nondiscrimination policy is not as consistent in its language, referencing 'gay and lesbian students' several times – including in their description of Hastings OUTLAW.

The same report also showed how bi erasure leaves bi organizations and initiatives under-funded, meaning that not only does bi erasure make it harder for bi people to find information and support, but those resources available are more limited than those for gay men and lesbians. 'In fact, during all of 2008, not a single grant in the entire country explicitly addressed bisexual issues,' the report noted, despite LGBT funding having increased in general. There was also no funding again in 2009 or 2010, as the LGBTQ Grantmaking fund report shows (Cunningham 2010).

The study 'Employment Discrimination Against Bisexuals and Others with Fluid Identities', which explores bi erasure in the legal field, goes a step further, suggesting that bisexuality is not only erased in litigation that protects sexual minorities, but is demonized in practice when persecuting a bi person, or to discredit a bi defendant. The study explains:

> Nonetheless, although bisexuals are the largest sexual minority group in the United States, electronically available court decisions involving bisexual plaintiffs' claims of employment discrimination are rare compared to those involving gay, lesbian, and heterosexual plaintiffs, and it seems to be virtually unheard of for a bisexual plaintiff to succeed in such a claim on the merits.
>
> Ironically, the most prominent appearance of bisexuals in employment discrimination case law is in the role of the so-called bisexual harasser, a largely hypothetical character who perpetrates discrimination with impunity because her treatment of both sexes is equally bad and therefore not actionable under Title VII. The confinement of bisexuals to this negative and largely hypothetical role in the case law may well be rooted in the popular stereotype that bisexuals are greedily attempting to have their cake and eat it too. (Tweedy and Yescavage 2013, pp.709–710)

This backs up Yoshino and others' claim that bi erasure is not an accident of a dominant binary worldview, but a tool wielded for unequal benefits for straight, and indirectly, gay people. When it is not possible to completely erase bisexuality, biphobic stereotypes are wielded against us instead.

BI THE WAY

Bi erasure is rampant in the LGBTIQ+ movement in

Australia. The mayor of Port Phillip Council, the host of Melbourne Pride March, gave a speech welcoming everyone to Pride but forgot to include bisexuals when listing the identities in the acronym. Also, the federal senator, first out lesbian in parliament, who has done the same thing several times. As well as that the whole marriage equality debate in Australia where we were erased and not included (though one of the anti-marriage equality religious groups used bi colours which was funny).

I can say that the marriage equality debate was definitely the most harmful with at least four known attempted suicides in the bi community in Melbourne (those that participated in the community at the time). When the so-called LGBTIQ marriage equality group makes a 'strategic' decision to erase bisexual, and trans and gender diverse people to make their argument 'easier' the harm reverberated across multiple communities. So many community groups, who were not consulted or engaged, were pissed with the way the Yes vote was framed and handled at the expense of bi and trans and gender diverse people.

Rebecca Dominguez

Intersectionality and bi erasure

Like biphobia, bi erasure isn't one size fits all. Those whose lives and experiences are invisibilized or under-represented because of other aspects of their identity such as race, ethnicity, class, disability, religion, or gender identity feel the effects of bi erasure more acutely because it is compounded by the erasure they already face. H. 'Herukhuti' Sharif Williams exemplified this by telling a story in his opening remarks of *Claiming the B in LGBT* (Harrad 2018) about learning that one of his friends is also bisexual, having previously assumed he was gay. He explains how a combination of monosexism and white supremacy forces black bisexuals to hide who they are, even in communities they belong to.

'I resisted the urge to question how I could have not recognised another Black bisexual man in all that time. How could I have? Like water, sexual fluidity often takes the shape of the container it inhabits. In gay spaces, we appear gay. In heterosexual spaces, we appear heterosexual. At least to others we do. Internally, we can be grappling with how not-quite-aligned we are with any those spaces as we attempt to form and maintain relationships. There is what always what feels like an overwhelming pressure of forces to conform,' he writes (Williams 2018, p.5).

So whilst combatting erasure will improve the lives and well-being of bi people in many ways, visibility isn't a cure-all. As well as fighting for better visibility, our community and allies need to also be focusing on eradicating biphobia and monosexism (which, as we've seen in Chapter 6 on history, has already been happening, and in the final chapter of this book, we'll explore some of the ways in which it is currently being tackled). Shiri Eisner explains:

> Reducing bisexual experience around oppression to the visual aspect only, necessarily means erasing all those other aspects of bisexual oppression that aren't perceived as visible or intuitive. As we've seen in chapter 2 [...] [T]his means most of them. Just to recall: Bisexuals experience oppression through cultural erasure, exploitation, marginalization, verbal, physical, and sexual violence, stereotyping, and internalized biphobia (just to name

a few), and in the fields of economics, employment, education, health, mental health, and interpersonal relationships (again, to name a few). (Eisner 2013a, p.101)

As well as this, any trans woman in the UK can tell you: hypervisibility can do a lot more harm than good. 'The received wisdom is that if people can see trans people they will learn to tolerate us, then to accept us and then to embrace us. I'm not convinced this sort of trickle-down liberation is enough. Firstly, the trans people who tend to be visible tend to be those judged as more palatable by media gatekeepers – younger, prettier, non-disabled and white,' wrote Shon Faye for the *Guardian*. Whilst this statement is about trans visibility, I think it also applies pretty well to the bi struggle for visibility (and of course, the two aren't mutually exclusive). She goes on: 'Trans representation in the media is one tactic, but it cannot replace trans people's full inclusion and participation in broader social movements like feminism, anti-racism and trade unionism.' Again, this is an approach I definitely advocate for the bi+ movement.

So now that we've delved into the mechanisms behind biphobia, monosexism, and bi erasure, let's take a look at what effects these have on the bi community in general.

CHAPTER 9

What Issues Do Bi People Face?

As we've explored over the last few chapters, the bi community experiences several types of marginalization and prejudice, including homophobia, biphobia, and monosexism. While it's sometimes hard to see the impact this has on individual bi people's lives, the picture becomes clear when we look at the wider community. In this chapter, we'll explore some of the key issues facing the bi community, breaking down the systems that enable them.

Mental health

Given how much bi people experience double discrimination, exclusion, and prejudice, it's no shock that bi people experience higher rates of mental health issues than our gay and straight counterparts. A study by Stonewall in 2018 found that 72 per cent of bi women had experienced issues with anxiety, compared to 60 per cent of lesbians (Bachmann and Gooch 2018). This trend was the same for bi men, 56 per cent of whom had experienced anxiety, compared to 53 per cent of gay men. While the study does show that 79 per cent of non-binary people had experienced anxiety, it does not break these findings down by orientation.

More worryingly, the study found that 'Bi people are more likely to have thought about taking their own life than lesbian and gay people, 41 per cent compared to 28 per cent.' Again, the trend of bi people having worse mental health outcomes continues when it comes to self-harm, with 28 per cent of bi women and 18 per cent of bi men saying they had self-harmed within the last year, compared to 14 per cent of lesbians and 7 per cent of gay men. In comparison, 6 per cent of the general public had reportedly self-harmed in the last year.

Another alarming statistic from the report is that *half* of bi women and 43 per cent of bi men reported that they felt like their life wasn't worth living in the last year, compared to 37 per cent of lesbians and 32 per cent of gay men responding in this way.

These statistics are in comparison to one in six adults in the general population who experience common mental health issues. In general, the study found that trans and non-binary people were more likely to experience mental health issues. The study also found that 'poor mental health is also higher among LGBT people who are young, Black, Asian or minority ethnic, disabled or from a socio-economically deprived background.' One particularly stark finding was that queer people of colour were twice as likely to have eating disorders than white LGBTQIA+ people.

While this study was focused on the UK, studies from other English-speaking countries have shown similar results. For example, a study from Australia found that '58% [of bi participants], reported either high or very high levels of psychological distress, with histories of anxiety, depression, and eating disorders the most common reported diagnoses. Almost half of the respondents disclosed self-harm or thoughts about suicide within just the last two years. More than one in four (28%) had attempted suicide in their lives and 78% had thought about it,' wrote *Psychology Today* in 2019 (Ley 2019). This study suggested that biphobia including internalized biphobia and lack of acceptance was one of the key factors behind these findings. Again, *Psychology Today* wrote, 'Interestingly, results did not find that having LGBTQ peers and friends was related to lower levels of biphobia or unhappiness' (Ley 2019).

Similarly, a study from San Francisco found that 'in nonurban areas, lesbians and bisexual women experience similar levels of frequent mental distress. However, while the odds of frequent mental distress decrease significantly for lesbians in urban areas, the odds nearly double for bisexual women' (Fredriksen-Goldsen et al. 2010). The researchers theorized that:

> In addition to the minority stressors encountered by lesbians, bisexual women may face stressors which may be associated with poor health outcomes, such as lack of support by lesbian and gay communities as well as the larger community. Urban environments are typically characterized as having more well-organized gay and lesbian communities; bisexual women in such environments may feel even more isolated because they do not have access to a defined community.

So, on top of the issues faced by all queer people due to marginalization, bi people are less likely to see mental health improvements after seeking out LGBTQIA+ communities due to the bi erasure and biphobia in those spaces. While I could not find any research confirming it, it seems likely that this issue is more pronounced for bi people of colour and disabled and trans bi people, who also face racism, ableism, and transphobia in LGBTQIA+ spheres, in addition to biphobia.

While bi people experience higher rates of mental illness, being bi in itself is not a mental illness and does not cause mental illness. The higher rates are due to bi people's experiences, not the orientation itself. While that might seem obvious, a lot of biphobes still think that being bi is a result or cause of neurosis or instability.

Physical health outcomes

As well as facing higher rates of mental health issues, the bi community also has worse physical health outcomes in many areas. This seems to be mostly due to lack of education around bi+ people's health needs, bi people not being out to healthcare workers, and the bi community being more likely to be dealing with issues that negatively affect one's health, such as living in poverty or dealing with addiction (we'll discuss both of these shortly).

The same Stonewall study quoted above found that while in general, one in five LGBT people were not out to their healthcare professionals, that number jumps to 40% for bi men and 29% for bi women.

Because of this, bi men are less likely to get tested for HIV. A study by the Centers for Disease Control and Prevention (CDC) in 2014 found that bi men experience higher rates of HIV than straight men. William Jeffries of the Division of HIV/AIDS at the CDC's National Center for HIV/AIDS, Viral Hepatitis, STD, and TB Prevention, who authored the study, wrote in the press statement:

Societal biphobia – negative attitudes and behaviors toward bisexual individuals – is more prevalent than antigay sentiment. It is sometimes perpetrated by lesbians and gay men, and public health professionals who interact with MSMW [men who have sex with men and women]. Biphobia can manifest in erroneous beliefs that MSMW are closeted gay men and, particularly for black men, responsible for HIV transmission to women. (Jeffries 2014)

A report by Human Rights Campaign, BiNet USA, Bisexual Resource Center and Bisexual Organising Project (n.d.) expands on the other health issues facing the bi community, saying:

Bisexuals face striking rates of poor health outcomes ranging from cancer…, to sexually transmitted infections to mental health problems.

Moreover, transgender people and people of color comprise large portions of the bisexual community – with more than 40 percent of LGBT people of color identifying as bisexual, and about half of transgender people describing their sexual orientation as bisexual or queer – making these groups vulnerable to further disparities that occur at the intersections of biphobia, racism and transphobia.

To help address this issue, the Bisexual Resource Center launched Bi Health Awareness Month in 2013. The initiative runs each March and aims to 'raise[s] awareness about the bisexual+ (bi, pansexual, fluid, queer, etc.) community's social, economic, and health disparities; advocates for resources; and inspires actions to improve bi+ people's well-being,' according to the 2020 Bi Health Awareness Month press release (Bisexual Resource Center n.d.-a).

Addiction

Multiple studies have shown that the bi community, particularly bi women, face higher rates of substance abuse than other demographics. The most recent study to suggest this found that:

> Both male and female sexual minority adults had significantly elevated rates of substance use compared to heterosexual adults. Furthermore, relative to lesbian/gay women, bisexual women had significantly elevated odds of binge drinking, marijuana use, illicit drug use, opioid misuse, and alcohol use disorder. (Schuler and Collins 2020)

Whilst there has been data showing this issue has been around for at least the past decade, only recently have researchers started looking into why (which is the first step into understanding how to address the issue). Researcher Megan S. Schuler (Schuler and Collins 2020) found that biphobia, trauma from sexual violence, and poverty can significantly increase bi women's risk. The study concludes:

> Potential contributing factors to the elevated substance use risk observed among bisexual women include both the cultural invisibility of bisexuality as well as stigma and negative stereotypes associated with bisexuality.

The study also suggested that a lack of resources for bi people as well as mental distress caused by biphobia and bi erasure may be factors contributing to bi women turning to cigarettes, alcohol, and drugs.

Poverty

Poverty is arguably one of the biggest issues facing the bi community, but it is also one of the most under-reported. The Center for American Progress found in 2018 that bisexual men are most likely to report a household income that falls below the poverty line, with almost a quarter of American bisexual men being poor, compared with 12 per cent of gay men and 6 per cent of straight men (Mirza 2018). The numbers were similar for bisexual women, with 21 per cent reporting living in poverty, compared with 14 per cent of straight women. Lesbians, on the other hand, were the least likely to be poor (the study did not break respondents down according to non-binary identities and/or people of colour).

The same study also found that bi people were less likely to currently be in work (53% of bi women were currently in work, compared to 76% of lesbians and 53% of straight women. And 61% of bi men reported being in work, compared to 70% of gay men and 78% of straight men). On top of that, bi people were more likely to be relying on public benefits, including Medicare. While this was also true for bi men, the difference was less significant. Reliance on Medicare could also be one factor in why bi people experience worse health outcomes, as they are less likely to be able to access private medical care, although there has not been any research into this yet. Finally, the study also found that bi women are as likely as straight women to be caring for children, which places a further financial strain on bi women.

The Williams Institute also found that bisexual people of color have especially high rates of participation in SNAP [Supplemental Nutrition Assistance Program]: 47% of African American bisexual people and 39% of 'other/multiracial' bisexual people are on food stamps (Gates 2014).

As well as this, a study from Rice University in Texas from

2015 found that 40 per cent of bisexual men and 42 per cent of bisexual women were living below the poverty line, compared to 25 per cent of straight men, 30 per cent of straight women, 23 per cent of gay men, and 25 per cent of lesbians (Gorman et al. 2015).

If bisexuals are minorities within the minority and experience unique and more extreme forms of discrimination, this might contribute to disparities in things like earnings, educational attainment, the propensity to smoke cigarettes and other factors that affect well-being,' Professor Bridget Gorman, author of the study, told PinkNews at the time (Payton 2015).

While there is very little research into this issue from other countries, there is some evidence from the UK to back up that this isn't just a problem faced by American bisexuals. A 2013 study by the University of Essex found that gay men and bisexual men and women in the UK are more likely to be poor than their heterosexual peers. Bisexual women experienced the greatest material disadvantage. The study states:

> Bisexual women are significantly more likely to report being behind with council tax payments and to be behind in paying some or all of household bills. In terms of state benefits, bisexual women are more likely in some instances to receive state benefits though none of these differences are statistically significant. Interestingly, bisexual women are significantly more likely to lack more consumer durables (specifically colour TVs, video or DVD players, tumble driers, and land-line telephones), and are significantly less likely to have the Internet or broadband as compared to heterosexual women. (Uhrig 2014, p.12)

The study goes on to explain:

> Bisexuals seem to have very similar household structures as

compared to heterosexuals yet...suffer health and earnings inequalities somewhat worse than gay men and lesbians which most likely contribute to their greater material disadvantage. (Uhrig 2014, p.12)

As well as these two studies, another from America found that bi+ university students were more likely to be going hungry or be food insecure than both their gay and straight counterparts. The study by Temple University and the Wisconsin HOPE Lab found that almost half of the 2000 bi students who took part in the study had experienced food and/or housing insecurity, compared to one-third of heterosexual students. The study also found that 'more than one in five bisexual community college students and 18% of homosexual community college students experienced homelessness, compared to 11% of their heterosexual peers' (Goldrick-Rab et al. 2018, p.19).

A recent study by the Human Rights Campaign (HRC) and PSB Insights also indicates that LGBTQIA+ plus people are more likely to have been affected by the Coronavirus pandemic as 'they are more likely to lack access to sufficient medical care, more likely to work in industries affected by the pandemic, and more likely to experience homelessness,' writes Forbes on the study (Sprayregen 2020). The report also found LGBTQIA+ were more likely to be laid off or have their hours cut. Forbes writes:

Since states began reopening, LGBTQ people have also been 30% more likely than the general population to lose their jobs, with the bisexual community being hit hardest.

Bisexual people have been 80% more likely to lose their jobs. LGBTQ people of color are also 70% more likely than the general population to have experienced job loss since states began reopening. (Sprayregen 2020)

Unsurprisingly, queer people of colour and trans individuals were also more acutely vulnerable to the impacts of Covid-19 and the 2020 lockdown (I specify 2020, because by time you read this, we may have had more. What a fun surprise that will be). To quote Forbes again, 'LGBTQ people of color and transgender people have been 44% and 125% more likely to experience a loss of hours, respectively' (Sprayregen 2020).

Homelessness

In general, queer people are more likely to experience homelessness than our straight peers: LGBTQIA+ people make up 24 per cent of the homeless population in the UK, according to the Albert Kennedy Trust (n.d.).

So, whilst this is an issue facing the whole community, evidence from America suggests the bi community might be more at risk. A study from the University of Nebraska–Lincoln found in 2016 that bisexuals make up 20 per cent of the homeless population in America (Whitbeck 2016). Not 20 per cent of LGBTQIA+ homeless people, 20 per cent of *all* homeless people. The study suggests that family rejection is the key factor behind LGBT people's increased risk of homelessness. As we saw in the previous section, poverty is also a big issue for the bi+ community, and this may play a role in our community's disproportionate rates of homelessness.

There is a strong link between homelessness and addiction, with addicts being more at risk of homelessness, and housing insecure people being more likely to abuse substances. 'During 2013–15, 27% of our clients reported problematic drug/alcohol use. Two thirds of homeless people cite drug or alcohol use as a reason for first becoming homeless. Those who use drugs are seven times more likely to be homeless,' writes the homeless charity, Crisis (2013).

Given that bi people experience higher rates of homelessness, addiction, and poverty, there could be a vicious circle of compounding problems stemming from biphobia that has yet to be researched or explored.

Education and employment barriers

The same study from the University of Essex quoted above found that bisexual students were significantly less likely to pursue A-levels than their gay, lesbian, and straight peers: 'about 55 percent aspire to get A-levels with similar results for those saying they have an "other" sexual orientation or prefer not to say,' the study says (Uhrig 2014, p.22).

Biphobic bullying is also rampant in schools, which may go some way to explain why bi pupils are less likely to want to continue education. A study from Northern Ireland, referred to in the University of Essex study, found that bi students were more at risk of being bullied:

Approximately 22 percent of heterosexual students experience any bullying – physical or otherwise – whereas nearly 38 percent of lesbian or gay students and 41 percent of bisexual students experience bullying. ... Bisexual students are particularly vulnerable to both physical and other kinds of bullying. (Uhrig 2014, p.25)

Evidence from across the pond suggests that the problem isn't isolated to the UK: a study conducted in America in 2011 found that nearly half of young bi people reported being bullied, compared to 20 per cent of straight youth and 30 per cent of lesbian and gay youth (Robinson and Espelage 2011).

In both countries, there is a pronounced lack of bi-specific resources available for pupils in schools. Stonewall found in 2017 that 76 per cent of students said they'd never learnt about or discussed bisexuality in school. On top of this, Stonewall's 'Celebrating Bi Inclusion in Secondary Schools' report notes that 'Bi pupils are less likely than lesbian and gay pupils to have an adult at home they can talk to about being LGBT (37 per cent compared to 46 per cent)', which is especially worrying given that 'One in three bi pupils (35 per cent) are bullied at school for being LGBT' (Stonewall 2018). In America, the HRC found in 2014 that bi students were less likely to know if their school has a GSA (Gay/Straight Alliance) or know of any LGBTQIA+ centres in the local area, compared to gay students (Andre 2014).

The bi community also faces similar barriers in the workplace. A 2015 study from America (which was open to international respondents) found that slightly over half of bisexual participants had experienced employment discrimination, with this number being significantly higher for bi people of colour (Tweedy and Yescavage 2015). The study found that being subjected to inappropriate jokes and comments was the most common type of discrimination experienced, followed by verbal harassment. The study concludes:

> These results corroborate existing research demonstrating that bisexuals are subject to both homophobia, largely from the mainstream culture, and biphobia, or oppression specifically linked to fear of bisexuals, which is perpetrated both by heterosexuals and lesbian and gay persons.

Bi erasure is another barrier in the workplace. As we've already seen, bi people are far less likely to be out than gay men and lesbians, meaning bi people have fewer openly bi role models to look up to in their workplaces or industries (and as the saying goes, you can't be what you don't see). On top of this, workplace LGBTQIA+ support networks are less likely to have bi-specific resources, and even if they do, the person may not feel they can access them at all. The 'Invisible Majority: The Disparities Facing Bisexual People and How to Remedy Them' report states:

A 2011 study by the Williams Institute found that only 6% of bisexual people reported being open about their sexual orientation to all their co-workers, compared to 40% of lesbian and gay people. A survey of LGBT Americans by the Pew Research Center found that only 11% of bisexual respondents reported their closest co-workers know that they are bisexual, while half of gay men and lesbians said that their co-workers know their sexual orientation. And only 44% of bisexual respondents said that their workplace is very accepting of bisexual people, compared to 60% of gay men and 50% of lesbians. (MAP 2016, p.10)

For bi people who exist on multiple axes of marginalization, such as race or disability, this invisibility and lack of support is even more pronounced. 'In all the places I worked that had these networks, they were almost always white and completely lesbian and gay only,' Jacq Applebee, the founder of Bis of Colour, an advocacy group for bisexual people from ethnic minorities, told me for an article in 2019. 'The experiences of a white gay man and that of a black bisexual femme are very different' (Shearing 2019).

The Williams Institute also notes that employment discrimination plays a factor in both minority stress, which has an impact on both physical and mental health, and earning potential, all issues which affect the bi community.

Asylum

Being granted asylum can mean the difference between life and death for LGBTQIA+ people who are fleeing persecution in their home country. As of 2020, 72 jurisdictions criminalize same-sex relationships, with over half of those countries being in the Commonwealth, and many of their laws being imported by the British and other European colonizers in the countries that aren't in the Commonwealth. There are currently eight countries in which same-sex relationships are punishable by death.

Whilst the process of seeking asylum is inhuman and degrading for all queer people (e.g., several people seeking asylum in the UK have had to resort to submitting videos of themselves having sex in order to prove their sexuality), bisexuals face unique barriers in the process.

Many asylum processes require proof that the claimant is gay, which is difficult to prove at the best of times, but impossible if you're not actually gay, because you're bi. In multiple cases, claimants' previous different-gender relationships have been used to deny their claims, with many bi (and gay) asylum seekers being told that they should return to their country of origin and pass as straight. Bi erasure means that bi asylum seekers may have their claims denied because officials don't believe bisexuality exists or because they believe that bi people can 'choose to be straight'. The Invisible Majority report shares an example of a bi man seeking asylum in America in 2016:

> Despite the asylum seeker's plethora of evidence documenting not only the years of physical harassment he endured in his country of origin, but also of his relationships with men and women, the immigration judge was skeptical of his bisexuality,

citing his wife and children as contrary evidence. As Judge Posner said in his dissent to the Seventh Circuit's ruling, 'The weakest part of the immigration judge's opinion is its conclusion that Fuller is not bisexual, a conclusion premised on the fact that he's had sexual relations with women (including a marriage). Apparently the immigration judge does not know the meaning of bisexual. (MAP 2016, p.12)

Because of this, some bi people have been encouraged to identify as gay when making asylum claims to increase their chances. Not only does this further erase the struggles and amount of bi asylum seekers, but it can also demean the claimant by implying their identity and experiences are less legitimate than a mono-sexual person's. As Apphia Kumar, the first person to be granted asylum in the USA on the basis of their bisexuality, wrote for GLAAD in 2017:

Everything online told me not to apply as bisexual, but to apply for asylum as a gay person. I've been mislabelled a lesbian in the past by over-excited journalists and people who thought they knew more about me than I did about my own identity, but this was different. I couldn't bring myself to even consider lying about who I am, after I had left my home because it was unsafe for me because of who I am. (Kumar 2017)

Data from the Home Office shows that the UK turned away two-thirds of gay and bi applicants between 2016 and 2018. Due to bi erasure, it is difficult to find data about just bi claimants, as these are not distinguished from gay claimants. However, several bisexual claimants have spoken out about their experiences, saying they face an environment of being considered gay in their home country but straight in their sought country of refuge.

In my opinion, this is one of the most clear-cut ways in which monosexism endangers bisexual people.

For example, Orashia Edwards sought refuge in the UK after being threatened with mob violence in Jamaica for having a relationship with a man. His case was originally denied, partially because he used to be married to a woman. During his two-and-a-half-year reprieve, Orashia's boyfriend tragically passed away, after which Orashia started dating a woman. Both he and his mother feared this would be used against him in his case. Thankfully, Orashia was granted asylum in 2016.

There is also very little scholarly research into the experiences and success rates of bisexual asylum seekers. However, one paper by Professor Sean Rehaag, Director of York University's Centre for Refugee Studies, found that bisexual people were also less likely to be granted asylum than gay men and lesbians in Canada, Australia, and America. Whilst there was not enough data available to draw decisive conclusions, Rehaag suggested that bi erasure and negative attitudes towards bisexuality within immigration courts may be factors. He writes:

> Reported refugee decisions reveal troubling views about bisexuality held by refugee claims adjudicators… Although explicit remarks involving such extremely negative views of bisexuality have been relatively rare in reported refugee decisions involving bisexuals, troubling views of bisexuality were nonetheless frequently implicit in the types of evidence that refugee claims adjudicators cited when assessing the sexual identities of refugee claimants. For example, in a Canadian case involving a woman from Iran, the IRB cited evidence that the claimant intended to marry a man to conclude that the claimant was not, in fact, a bisexual. (Rehaag 2009)

In a more extreme case, Rehaag found that a young bisexual girl was denied asylum in Canada because she has reportedly not been sexually active whilst in the country. Having reportedly been sexually active with both men and women in her native Iran, the judge believed that 'the claimant testified that she has not been sexually active [in Canada]. She [says she] is under-age to go to gay clubs and she is busy with going to school. It is difficult to believe how a person sexually active with a male and two females from the age of 14 is living a celibate life now,' so she must therefore be lying. This attitude reflects the biphobic notion that bi women are hypersexual and controlled by our sexual urges.

Sexual and intimate partner violence

The bi community, especially women, face higher rates of sexual and intimate partner violence than our gay or straight peers. Studies from the UK, America, Canada, and Europe suggest that this is a widespread issue facing bi people, rather than an issue in just one society.

A study from the Office for National Statistics (2018) in the UK found that bi women are twice as likely as straight women to have experienced partner abuse in the past 12 months, and nearly *five times* as likely to have experienced sexual assault from a partner or ex-partner. The study also found that women from mixed ethnicity were most likely to have experienced intimate partner violence.

In America, the CDC found in 2010 that 'bisexual women had significantly higher lifetime prevalence of rape and sexual violence other than rape by any perpetrator when compared to both lesbian and heterosexual women' (Walters, Chen, and

Breiding 2013, p.1), as well as significantly higher lifetime prevalence of intimate partner stalking. Shockingly, the study found that the lifetime prevalence of 'sexual violence other than rape (including being made to penetrate, sexual coercion, unwanted sexual contact, and non-contact unwanted sexual experiences) by any perpetrator' (p.1) for bi women was 74.9 per cent, compared to 46.4 per cent for lesbians and 43.3 per cent for heterosexual women. Whilst the rates were lower for men, bi men were still most at risk: 47.4 per cent for bi men compared to 40.2 per cent for gay men and 20.8 per cent for straight men. The study did not include data for non-binary people, nor did it clarify the trans status of participants.

Overall, the study found that the lifetime prevalence of experiencing intimate partner violence, including rape, assault, physical violence, and stalking, was 61.1 per cent for bi women, compared to 43.8 per cent for lesbians, and 35.0 per cent for straight women. For men, the prevalence was 37.3 per cent for bi men, 26.0 per cent for gay men, and 29.0 per cent for straight men.

Seven years later, in 2017, researcher Dr Nicole Johnson, of the Department of Education and Human Services at Lehigh University, put forward three factors that might contribute to bi women's increased risk: hypersexualization, biphobic harassment, and substance use (Johnson 2017).

'The media, and pornography in particular, have long depicted women's bisexuality as less about sexual agency and more about the pleasure of straight men, which may result in the dehumanisation and objectification of bisexual women resulting in increased acceptance of violence [against them],' Dr Johnson told me for an article in 2018 (Shearing 2018b). She also suggests that biphobic harassment, or biphobia, helps to normalize violence against bi women. Stereotypes that bi women can't be trusted create environments of jealousy and controlling behaviour against bi women in intimate relationships.

As we've seen already, bi women are more likely to experience addiction and substance misuse, which can place us in more vulnerable situations. That's not to say that any type of violence is because of substance abuse or even because of the victim's bisexuality itself. The violence is always, solely, the aggressor's fault.

A 2018 report from the United Nations went as far as to describe the rates of sexual violence against bi women as 'shocking', going on to say that 'bisexual women are especially at risk of acts of sexual or intrafamily and domestic violence' (United Nations General Assembly 2018, p.11).

As with other issues facing the bi community, especially addiction, education/employment discrimination, and asylum, individuals who exist on multiple axes of oppression face an even higher prevalence of sexual/intimate partner violence. As we saw in previous chapters, bisexuals of colour, particularly black women, are especially vulnerable to sexual violence, as they are hypersexualized for both their race and sexuality. Trans, non-binary, and gender non-conforming bi people are also at higher risk. The Invisible Majority report explains:

> Among transgender and gender non-conforming students responding to a survey by the Association of American Universities, bisexual transgender and gender non-conforming students reported the highest rate of experiencing nonconsensual sexual contact involving physical force or incapacitation: 24% of bisexual transgender and gender non-conforming students, compared to 9% of heterosexual transgender and gender non-conforming students and 18% of lesbian and gay transgender and gender non-conforming students. (MAP 2016, p.20)

On top of all of this, some studies have shown that bi people are more likely to report negative experiences when reporting or seeking support. The Invisible Majority report also explains:

> When reporting sexual assault, bisexual women receive the fewest positive social reactions, compared to lesbian and heterosexual women. In fact, the National LGBTQ Domestic Violence Capacity Building Learning Center held a series of focus groups with bisexual women survivors of domestic violence and found that bisexual women felt that their abusive partners were threatened by their sexuality and used that as a reason for perpetuating violence. Bisexual women reported 'going back into the closet' as a survival mechanism when experiencing intimate partner violence as their bisexual identity was seen as threatening to abusive partners. And finally, bisexual women survivors reported feeling isolated from LGBTQ people and from the broader community and often did not disclose their bisexual identity when accessing services for intimate partner violence. (MAP 2016, p.20)

It is for these reasons that I founded the Bi Survivors Network. I couldn't find the right kind of support from mainstream organizations, which treated LGBTQIA+ survivors as homogeneous, and LGBTQIA+-focused survivor support often assumes that the intimate partner violence took place within a same-gender relationship. When accessing either, there is a risk of facing biphobia, invasive questioning, and lack of understanding. I and the rest of the BSN team have heard many stories about people's negative experiences with other survivor services from the people who come to us looking for a space where they won't have to explain or defend their identity.

As we've discussed in previous chapters, the bi community is the most under-funded, under-researched, and under-supported beneath the LGBTQIA+ umbrella, with many of these issues going unaddressed by the very organizations that claim to represent us. But that doesn't mean that these issues are going completely ignored; the bi community ourselves continues to fight tooth and nail to support each other. In the next and final chapter (thanks for making it this far!) we'll take a broad look at what the bi movement has achieved, where it is, and perhaps most importantly, where it's going.

CHAPTER 10

What's the Bi Community Like and How Do I Find It?

U nless you skipped straight to this chapter (which is fair enough, you know what you want), you've probably got the point that no matter how much society tries to erase and suppress us, the bi community continues to fight, love, argue, scheme, succeed, party, create, celebrate, and, well, *exist*.

Because of bi erasure, people frequently don't know what to look for when they begin searching for resources and support. Lots of bi people end up settling for feeling like an afterthought in gay-focused settings, and some even end up re-closeting themselves or living with perceived isolation in the heterosexual world.

But I'm here to tell you that those aren't the only options. A rich bi scene of culture, memes, meetups, apps, artists, activists, and friends is abubble just under the surface of the mainstream LGBTQIA+ community and the world in general. There will be bi communities you can join in your area or that suit your interests, and if none fits your needs, other bi activists, organizers, and community leaders will be *more* than willing to help you create your own.

It's also important to remember that there isn't just one homogeneous bi+ community. Any time when a group of bi+ people get together, whether as friends, activists, academics, performers, or whatever, that is its own bi community. Bi communities in the West are going to have a different culture, objectives, and traditions from bi communities in the Majority World. Bi communities for people of colour, or disabled bi people, or trans bi people are going to be different to more generalized bi groups, because a community is the collective of each person's experiences and the history of the community. So American bi culture and communities will differ from British ones, which will differ from European ones, etc., all the way down, even from city to city. So if you don't feel that your experiences of bi culture or community is represented in this chapter, it doesn't mean you're not really bi or part of that community, it just means your community has its own unique culture, and unfortunately, I'm not able to cover them all.

BI THE WAY

The bi+ community has meant an immeasurable amount to me – it's been where I've met most of my friends and all of my partners for more than 25 years. It's been a constant reassurance that it's okay to be myself, to be bisexual, and to continue to discover more about myself as I get older. It's where I found the confidence to speak out, and speak up. And I've found that the way to get the most out of the community is to put energy into it – to be useful to the bisexual+ community. As the years have gone by, I've therefore not found myself needing it less, just needing it in different ways. It's been said that one of the first jobs for activists is training our successors, and that's how I

> want to be useful to the community now, through things like The Bisexual Index and activist training.
>
> *Marcus Morgan, bi+ activist, performer,*
> *and director of The Bisexual Index*

There are dozens of groups and resources in the UK and around the world working to create spaces and resources for bi people, as well as fighting for our rights and protection, and combatting bi erasure. To get you started in your search, here's a few examples:

- **The Bisexual Index** – provides useful information and contains a directory of other bi+ groups.
- **Bis of Colour** – a support and advocacy group for black, Asian, and minority ethnicity bi+ people.
- **Biscuit** – an advocacy group for bi+ women.
- **Bi Pride UK** – an organization working to increase bi visibility and create more safe spaces for the bi+ community at Prides around the country.
- **Bi Survivors Network** – a group that provides support and advocacy for bi+ survivors of sexual or domestic violence.
- **bWithTheT** – a banner under which bi and trans people can organize in solidarity.
- **Bi Community News** – the UK's only bi+ print magazine.

BI THE WAY

The lack of much cultural commentary on the bi+ experience specific to India (as of concrete academic work theorizing the same), and what there is being subsumed under the label of 'LGBTQ' or 'queer' makes it hard to find knowledge and representation for those seeking it. Unfortunately, in our context, 'queerness' often also lends itself to bi erasure. The bi+ community is consequently very atomized and marginalized.

The predominant form of the family system in South Asia is the heteronormative marriage with a high degree of regulation of sexuality, especially for women. The prevalence of arranged marriages often makes it difficult for bi people to find the full expression of their identity within those structures. A lot of people reaching out to us for support are living within this form of companionship that may not have been of their choosing or that they felt compelled to get into earlier than they might have liked to. Another big challenge is conversion 'therapy' – a form of institutionalized violence which has been discredited by several associations of Indian psychiatrists and psychologists.

The reaction to our group has been overwhelmingly positive. There is a recognized need for bi+ support groups and resource groups like the one we are, and given that we are completely voluntary and independent, that makes it especially valuable as a peer-support network. Being part of the larger bi+ community is integral to our understanding of bisexuality as a potentially radical form of emancipatory politics which is founded in identities based on different forms of non-monosexual attraction. We hope the bi+ movement takes off in a more confident way in Asia, and that it comes into its own as a distinct movement in solidarity with different groups belonging to the LGBTQ+ spectrum.

The Bi Collective Delhi

These are just the groups operating on a national level. As of the time of writing, Biscuit lists 28 regional bi groups around the UK, mostly dedicated to community and socializing. Beyond our little island, there are bi groups all over the world, with many in America and in Europe, but more popping up every year, including:

- **Bi.org** – a news and opinion site, written and curated by the bi+ community and the American Institute of Bisexuality.
- **Bisexual Resource Center** – a resource collective that aims to 'connect the bi+ community and help its members thrive through resources, support, and celebration'.
- **The Bi Collective Delhi** – India's first bi+ group; a resource and support group for bi+ people in the country.
- **Bigruppen** – the largest bi+ community group in Denmark, organizing theme nights, dances, Pride groups, and more.
- **Bi-naiset** – a bi+ feminist group in Helsinki.
- **Bisexualite.info** – a French-language website that provides resources for bi+ people and facilitates discussions.
- **Bisexuelles Netzwerk (BiNe)** – Germany's bisexual network.
- **KVartIR** – a group advocating for visibility, networking, and raising awareness of bisexual, transgender, and asexual identities in Slovenia.
- **Biszkopty** – possibly Poland's only bi+ group and something we as a community must work to protect and support as anti-LGBTQIA+ violence rises in that country.
- **Bi+ Oceania** – a bi+ community group bringing together resources and 'promoting equal rights and wellbeing for people who are attracted to more than one gender' for people in Australia, New Zealand, and the Pacific Islands.

- **#StillBisexual** – an organization that started out as a social media campaign helping bi+ people tell their stories, it is now working to provide 'education and health advocacy'.

And many, many, many, *many* more. While the bi community might be erased and critically under-funded, it's definitely there, providing support and resources and solidarity all over the world. The majority of these groups are run by volunteers on shoestring budgets, because as we already discussed, bi organizations receive the least amount of funding of any LGBTQIA+-focused ventures. For example, in 2013 the annual Funders for LGBT Issues report, which tracks private funding for LGBTQIA+ causes, found that bi+ focused initiatives received less than 1 per cent of that year's funding: $475,000 out of $129 million (Kan and Maulbeck 2013). This is especially shocking given that bi+ people make up the majority of the queer community. Even more shockingly, in 2016, the bi+ community only received $300 of funding, despite overall funding for queer issues surpassing $2 million for the first time. In the most recent report from 2017/18, bi causes still received less than 1 per cent. So, while the bi+ community has continued to make great strides in our fight for better visibility, it doesn't yet seem to have translated into cold, hard cash.

BI THE WAY

What the UK bisexual community is, and what I wish it would be, are two very different things. I wish the community was inclusive of ethnicity and race. I wish they would learn from their mistakes, or simply just learn about making things better – without demanding Black and People of Colour to teach them. I wish I felt welcome in the white-majority bisexual community.

When a few friends and I started Bis of Colour in 2010, we wanted a space where we didn't have to censor ourselves for fear of retribution. We wanted a space where we could celebrate and mourn all that is bisexuality in a Brown and Black body. Over the years we have made friends and contacts with other bisexuals of colour groups in countries including the Philippines, Brazil, and India. We have listened to echoes of our lives and experiences. We have formed a global community where we aren't treated like freaks or a square on a white person's sexual bingo card. We have found each other at last: a bisexual community for all of us.

Jacq Applebee, co-founder of Bis of Colour

On previous occasions when I've brought up this issue of funding, people have accused me of wanting to take away money from other very deserving causes for gay men, lesbians, trans people, ace people, and others in the community in general. That's definitely not the case; I'm advocating that instead of giving bisexuals a bigger slice of the pie, we demand a bigger pie. We demand as much pie as we need. Infinite pie. And we use that pie to help support our communities while we fight for a world where queer people don't need to have a specific pie, or even a world where pie doesn't exist.

This lack of funding, as well as facing biphobia when trying to organize with other LGBTQIA+ organizations, means that resources and community support for bi people can sometimes be patchy and inconsistent, and our fight for better visibility and equality has been far from linear. For example, in 2017, there was not going to be any bi+ presence in Pride in London. Then, in 2018 there was the First Bi Pride Float and two walking groups. By 2019, there was a float and three walking groups (including my own BWithTheT marching group). But, as London Bi Pandas, who organized 2019's float, shuttered in 2020, it's unclear what presence the bi+ community will have at Pride in London in 2021.

On top of this, the bi+ community has always been defined by a transience and fluidity, which is reflected in our events, meetings, and culture. Bi events and campaigns are often ad hoc and created as a reaction to an event (e.g. the First Bi Pride Float was a reaction to there being no bi+ presence the year before). In the report *Embracing the 'And': Between Queer and Bi Theory at Brighton BiFest*, Georgina Voss, Kath Brown, and Camel Gupta (2014) write:

> Yet [bi+ events/communities] are temporally specific; by creating a fixed bi identity category for a specific time period, the label of bi can be seen as a temporary performance to be embraced and staged for the purposes of a singular event with a particular purpose, rather than a permanent limiting label.

In this report, Voss et al. suggest that the ephemeral nature of bi spaces is not just a result of lack of funding or support, but a reflection of the bi+ politics of creating space to push back against bi+ negativity, without creating a fixed bi 'identity' that might exclude some members of our community. I have previously said (often when I've had a glass of wine and I'm feeling pretentious) that the reason I lean so much into bi politics and activism isn't that I'm very attached to being attracted to all genders, but because it's a space where my fluid and ambiguous sense of self can flourish. I'm a big fan of phases and I've had many; I pick up and put down interests and identities and aesthetics regularly. That's not to say that bisexuality is a phase, – of course, it isn't – but bi spaces have always been somewhere where my lack of permanence in things like my gender, interests, and desires is not questioned. Also, even if bisexuality is a phase for some, that doesn't make it less valid for others, or even for that person. For me, bisexuality has always meant the possibility of multiplicity, in both my partners and self. Voss et al. (2014) continue:

> From its inception, the events and technologies of the UK bisexual community have been characterized by ephemerality, while also challenging the notion of a single fixed identity. When the movement emerged in the early 1980s (Lano, 1995), it drew on a collection of existing identities and communities, including the men's anti-sexist movement, the women's movement, and the lesbian and gay movement.

That's not to say there are no regular bi+ events or spaces. In the UK we have several, including the annual BiCon, the UK's biggest bisexual convention. BiCon started in 1984 and since then it's been held in a different location around the country every summer. Over the four days, there is a mix of workshops, talks, and socials. The event culminates in the UK's biggest bi disco.

'BiCon was the first time I'd been around hundreds of people who didn't judge me for my sexuality, they loved me for it,' says Sali Owens, a bisexual activist. She then went on to run the UK's first year-long programme for bi youth facilitated by a charity. 'People from all over the country had the experience I had at my first BiCon and it was beautiful,' she says.

Because of the aforementioned biphobia in both queer and mainstream spaces, and the general heternormativity of our society, being in a space where you feel like your whole self and sexuality is finally accepted, without needing to hide or minimize any part of yourself for the first time, is a powerful experience.

BI THE WAY

Without a very vocal and accepting bisexual community online, I doubt I ever would have felt strong in my identity or my activism. I feel like I have a strong group of bisexual people around me now who are truly supportive. During my own journey as an activist, I have found myself engaging with lots of bisexual women who are finally feeling confident in their sexuality. This truly brings me so much joy as I know I represent a very fluid kind of bisexuality and it took me a while to feel comfortable in that myself. I like to know I could possibly be helping people explore aspects of themselves which they had once locked away in a box.

I do however, feel that we need to truly address bisexual mental health more within our community, alongside bi erasure. Bisexual people have always been part of the LGBTQ+ community and the consistent erasure alongside the discrimination is utterly detrimental to our mental health. I hope that, moving forward, there can truly be a push to focus on the specific issues bisexual people currently face. I do have hope that these conversations will be had more openly in the future and I feel like I am seeing these changes slowly happening.

Essie Dennis – LGBTQ+ activist and influencer

As well as BiCon in the UK, there's also EuroBiCon, which began in 2001 but took a 15-year hiatus, returning in 2016 and running annually for 3 years. As of writing this in 2020, there has not been another EuroBiCon because the whole world went into shutdown.

Then there's BiFest, an annual one-day event that takes place in London. Like BiCon, the day is made up of a mix of workshops, talks, and social events. Over the last few years, I've been lucky enough to run a cross-stitch workshop as part of my bi sewing group, Stitch Bi Stitch. In years' time, historians will wonder why so many bi+ people in London could suddenly cross-stitch and knit, and they will have me and my two amazing Stitch Bi Stitch co-hosts to thank. There's also London Bi Meetup, which hosts regular social events in London, and BiPhoria, the UK's longest-running bi organization, which organizes support and social events in Manchester. 'I struggled alone with feelings of "Am I really bi enough?" for 6 years, then found an in-real-life bi support group (BiPhoria) and within two visits, realised that my insecurities were due to social biphobia not me being a "bad" bisexual. It was life-changing,' Emily Write, who identifies as bisexual, told me on Twitter.

BI THE WAY

What I hope to see from the bi+ community is our collective energy put into creating resources & community for ourselves, and less energy put into begging the broader queer community to accept us. I think it's still important to call out biphobia & demand inclusion, but every bi person I know is exhausted by that being the focus. The nastiness doesn't go away if we ignore it, but maybe if we can build more solid & broad community resources, it'll be easier for adults to bear and bi youth would have somewhere to go other than LGBTQ+ organizations who give us 1–2% of their attention. I see a ton of this work happening in our generation, and more online resources popping up! But in real life bi resources in my experience still have a long long long way to go, when they exist at all, and I hope to see that improve in my lifetime. None of that is to discount work already done by bi activists for the past several decades. It just seems right now it is EXTREMELY easy for especially baby bis to get caught up in this recursive begging-people-not-to-be-mean game and getting no further than that because it's so emotionally devastating.

When I think about bisexuality, I think about *potential*, we are potential personified, and there is endless possibility for the bi community when we band together and take care of each other. Even more so when we team up with pansexual folks!

Bren, disabled bi+ advocate

Thanks to social media, it's easier than ever to create groups like Stitch Bi Stitch, and there are several bi-oriented groups on Meetup and other event platforms. As well as facilitating in-person groups, the internet is awash with digital bi communities. A search for bi groups on Facebook returns dozens of results, ranging from the generic like those for solidarity, culture, and exposing biphobia, to the niche-est of niche, including having angry thighs, and even bi witches. You also find a lot of groups about Power BI, which is apparently a business analysis tool and not anything to do with very strong bis, as I was hoping.

There are also multiple subreddits dedicated to bisexuality and of course 'bi Tumblr'. 'Finding bi Tumblr in, like, 2012 probably saved my life. I got involved with BIWOC [Bi Women of Colour, a community on Tumblr] before it was archived and I'm still friends with the founder,' says bisexual poet and author Maz Hedgehog. Tumblr is also where I first started to dip my toes into the world of bi activism and academia. Whilst the amount of misinformation is partially what inspired me to start writing about bi issues, it was also the first place that showed me that bi people had our own history and culture and didn't have to stand for being treated like the gay communities' annoying younger sibling who's crashing their sleepover.

BI THE WAY

I came into the bi activism sphere in early 2017 from more general queer activism, and it definitely feels like there's been a lot of change in even that relatively short time, with more spaces and groups popping up across the UK all the time. Much of the time it definitely seems like bi activists and bi communities are shouting into a wider space that is determined to ignore us, but on at least a micro-level my impression is that more and more general lG(bt) charities and professional networks are waking up to the fact that bi (and trans) experiences can't just be lumped together with those of cisgender gay people and taking baby steps towards building that into their programming and communications. It's nowhere near enough, and nowhere near fast enough, and it's very rarely adequately financially resourced, but it's at least the right direction! And I hope that the work Bi Pride UK has done has been able to contribute towards that growth of spaces and volume of voices.

Looking forwards, there are two key things that I hope

to see more of in bi activism. The first is the eternal desire: more funding for bi-specific work. The model that we as a registered charity have been able to put to corporates has been very appealing, in terms of event sponsorship which comes with bi inclusion training for their workplace, and we're gradually fielding more requests for delivering stand-alone training across the sectors (charity, public, and corporate), but we've as yet had limited success in securing funding through trusts and foundations, which I suspect is going to be the most reliable source of funding as the financial crunch of the pandemic makes itself more and more felt over the coming years. I hope to see grant funders really beginning to recognize the need to designate money specifically to work for bi communities.

What this year's pandemic has also underlined is the importance of virtual spaces in queer communities. With bi people more likely to be isolated, experience mental health issues, experience physical barriers to participation, and be living under the poverty line and/or in unstable employment, online spaces that are available from within the home (and even from bed if needed) and allow ways to be fully immersed in community without having to go somewhere to find it are vital. Bi communities have always known this and have always had this, but as we adapt to the potential longer-term impacts of coronavirus, it's going to be really important that we find more ways to build virtual participation into physical events and think consciously about how to bring the people who aren't in the room into the room in different ways. It's certainly something we plan to think more about for future Bi Pride events!

Avi Kay, chair of Bi Pride UK

Social media has hugely amplified bi visibility, capitalizing on the three decades of activism that preceded it. This increased visibility has led to young people exploring what makes up bi culture. Back in 1978, Klein had already predicted this rise in a hunger for a bisexual culture, writing: 'bisexual subculture would be yet another dimension of bisexual life, but if there is such a subculture it is too small to have any perceptible significance. With increased media focus on bisexuality, we will probably see a new subculture develop, as bisexuals increase the frequency of their mutual interaction, and discover the extent to which they are a special group with beliefs and behavior different from those of other people' (Klein [1978] 2014, pp.21–22).

Like all subcultures, bi culture is pretty hard to pin down. Given that subcultures are defined as a set of values or norms that run counter to or differ from those held by the majority, you could argue that being bi in itself is a subculture, as it runs counter to the widely held norm of monosexuality. But bi culture isn't just our shared desires and sexuality, it's made up of so many things from our shared experience of existing in a world that rejects both our same-gender and multi-gender attraction. If we were to take a cold, hard look at that experience, bi culture is pretty bleak; it's high rates of depression, addiction, and poverty. But it's so much more than that, it's also made of parts of our communities' resilience, strength, and compassion as we fight against our marginalization.

BI THE WAY

[Bi culture is] the culture of being hated and rejected by both the 'normal' heterosexual world and LGBT community yet still fighting for the rights and prosperity of all. We are, at our core, activists.

Anonymous

Bi culture is made up of so many things from our shared history, present, and future. It's puns, not sitting right, cuffing your jeans, negative capability, pandas, sweet and salty popcorn, side shaves, the bi bob, starter and dessert, ear tattoos, pastel colours (especially on floats and parade blocks), embracing the power of 'and', pink-purple-blue themed everything, tie-dye, leather jackets, Doc Martens and Vans, emo, drag, having a crush on the entire cast of a movie, finger guns, Panic! At The Disco, tucking in your top, eyeliner, vampy makeup, double denim, vampires, being ironically indecisive, Wonder Woman, bi lighting, '80s music, skating, owning the month of September, lemon bars, and, of course, declaring anything and everything as 'bi culture'.

That's not to say that these things are exclusively bi, of course. Many aspects overlap with lesbian, gay, trans, and ace culture. And you don't have to relate to any of them to be bi. But the bi community deserves so much more than only to be defined by our erasure and shared prejudice. Any group that is united by such an important aspect of identity will begin to develop shared aesthetics, customs, and even in-jokes. For lesbians there's plaid, U-Hauling, and 'Harold, they're lesbians'. For gay men it's camp, walking fast, and iced coffee. For trans people it's transition timelines, choosing your own name, and every third person being a developer. One of the things I'm most excited for as a bi person and an activist is to see how our culture develops as we increase in visibility and connectedness, especially when I see what young people are creating and doing.

> **BI THE WAY**
>
> [Bi culture is] being made to feel unwelcome among queer
> spaces and non queer spaces so you go out of your way
> to make sure people feel welcome because you know how
> much it sucks.
>
> *August Cotter*

While we still face a long journey and struggle, especially given
the state of the sociopolitical landscape as I sit writing this in
2020, I have a lot of hope for the bi+ community. We continue to
fight and love, and I'm constantly seeing new and inventive ways
in which we are advocating for each other and ourselves. From
coming-out TikToks, to vigils, protests, online support groups,
memes, articles, videos, rallying, performing, creating, archiving,
and connecting, we are constantly evolving our understanding
of ourselves and our needs. I think I speak for the whole bi+
community when I say: I can't wait to see where your journey
takes you and what you'll do.

References

Alexa, G. (n.d.). *Why Butch/Femme Belong to Bisexuals as Well.* [online] shopbigirlsclub.com. Available at: https://shopbigirlsclub.com/why-butch-femme-belong-to-bisexuals-as-well-and-bi-history-resources

Amherst, M. (2018). *Go the Way Your Blood Beats: On Truth, Bisexuality and Desire.* London: Repeater Books.

Andre, A., Brown, J., Delpercio, A., Kahn, E., Nicoll, A., and Sherouse, B. (2014). *Supporting and Caring for Our Bisexual Youth.* Washington, D.C.: The Human Rights Campaign Foundation.

Angelides, S. (2001). *A History of Bisexuality.* Chicago, IL: University of Chicago Press.

Antjoule, N. (2013). *The Hate Crime Report.* [online] Galop. Available at: www.galop.org.uk/wp-content/uploads/2013/08/The-Hate-Crime-Report-2013.pdf

Avery, E. (1993). SBWN: The Personal and the Political. *North Bi Northwest,* 5(6), 1.

Bachmann, C.L. and Gooch, B. (2017). *LGBT in Britain: Hate Crime and Discrimination.* [online] Stonewall. Available at: www.stonewall.org.uk/system/files/lgbt_in_britain_hate_crime.pdf

Bachmann, C.L. and Gooch, B. (2018). *LGBT in Britain: Health Report.* [online] Stonewall. Available at: www.stonewall.org.uk/system/files/lgbt_in_britain_health.pdf

Barker, M.-J. and Iantaffi, A. (2019). *Life Isn't Binary: On Being Both, Beyond, and In-Between.* London: Jessica Kingsley Publishers.

Baxter-Williams, L. (2015). *Hoisting Our Colours: A Brief History of the Bisexual Pride Flag.* [online] Biscuit. Available at: www.thisisbiscuit.co.uk/hoisting-our-colours-a-brief-history-of-the-bisexual-pride-flag

Bindel, J. (2012). *Where's the Politics in Sex?* [online] HuffPost. Available at: www.huffpost.com/entry/where-is-the-politics-in-_b_1589435

BiNet USA (2014). *BiNet USA's Blog: 1990 Anything that Moves Bisexual Manifesto.* [online] Accessed on 01/08/2019 at: http://binetusa.blogspot.com/2014/01/1990-bi-manifesto.html

BiNet USA (2016). *BiNet USA's Blog: Correct the Definition of Bisexuality on Dictionary.com to Reflect the Bisexual Community's Definition.* [online] Accessed on 01/08/2019 at: http://binetusa.blogspot.com/2016/02/correct-definition-of-bisexuality-on.html

Bi-Privilege.tumblr (n.d.). *Bi Privilege.* [online] Available at: https://bi-privilege.tumblr.com/idingasbipolyorpan

Bi.org. (n.d.-a). *Bi People Have Yet to Rise.* [online] Available at: https://bi.org/en/articles/bi-people-have-yet-to-rise

Bi.org. (n.d.-b). *The AIB Model.* [online] Available at: https://bi.org/en/101/AIB-model

bisexualindex.org.uk. (n.d.). *Am I Bisexual?* [online] Bisexual Index. Available at: http://bisexualindex.org.uk/index.php/AmIBisexual

Bisexual Resource Center. (n.d.-a). *Bisexual Health Awareness Month.* [online] Available at: https://bihealthmonth.org

Bisexual Resource Center. (n.d.-b). Coming Out as Bi+. [online] Available at: https://biresource.org/coming-out-as-bi

Bisexual Resource Center. (n.d.-c). *What Is Bisexuality?* [online] Available at: https://biresource.org/bi-info/youth/what-is-bisexuality

Bliss, N. (1995). Why You Must Say 'and Bisexual'. In Tucker, N., L.A. Highleyman and R. Kaplan (eds), *Bisexual Politics: Theories, Queries, and Vision.* New York: Harrington Park Press.

Bradlow, J., Bartram, F., Guasp, A., and Jadva, V. (2017). *School Report: The Experiences of Lesbian, Gay, Bi and Trans Young People in Britain's Schools in 2017.* [online] Stonewall. Available at: www.stonewall.org.uk/system/files/the_school_report_2017.pdf

Brooks, X. (2017, 9 March). *Kristen Stewart: 'It's Not Confusing if You're Bisexual. For Me, It's the Opposite'.* [online] The Guardian. Available at: www.theguardian.com/film/2017/mar/09/kristen-stewart-bisexual-personal-shopper-trump-tweets

Burston, P. (2012, 16 September). *Bisexuality in the Workplace: LGBT Networks Aren't Enough.* [online] The Guardian. Available at: www.theguardian.com/careers/bisexuality-in-workplace-lgbt-networks

Butler, J. (1993). *Bodies That Matter: On the Discursive Limits of 'Sex'.* London: Routledge.

Cantarella, E. (2002). *Bisexuality in the Ancient World.* [online] New Haven, CT: Yale University Press.

Chamberlain, B. (2012). *Bisexual People in the Workplace: Practical Advice for Employers.* [online] Stonewall. Available at: www.stonewall.org.uk/sites/default/files/bisexual_people_workplace.pdf

Crisis. (2013). *Drugs and Alcohol.* [online] Available at: www.crisis.org.uk/ending-homelessness/health-and-wellbeing/drugs-and-alcohol

Cruz, E. (2014). *When Bisexual People Get Left Out of Marriage.* [online] *The Advocate.* Available at: www.advocate.com/bisexuality/2014/08/26/when-bisexual-people-get-left-out-marriage

Cunningham, N. (2010). *Lesbian, Gay, Bisexual, Transgender and Queer Grant-making by U.S. Foundations.* [online] Funders for LGBT Issues. Available at: https://lgbtfunders.org/wp-content/uploads/2018/04/2010LGBTQGrantmakingReport.pdf

Dodge, B., Herbenick, D., Friedman, M.R., Schick, V., Fu, T.-C., Bostwick W., et al. (2016) Attitudes Toward Bisexual Men and Women Among a Nationally Representative Probability Sample of Adults in the United States. PLoS ONE 11(10), e0164430.

Donaldson, S. (1995). The Bisexual Movement's Beginnings in the 70s: A Personal Retrospective. In Tucker, N., L.A. Highleyman and R. Kaplan (eds), *Bisexual Politics: Theories, Queries, and Vision.* New York: Harrington Park Press.

Eisner, S. (2013a). *Bi: Notes for a Bisexual Revolution.* Berkeley, CA: Seal Press.

Eisner, S. (2013b). *The Difference Between Monosexism and Biphobia.* [online] Bi Radical. Available at: https://radicalbi.wordpress.com/2013/02/08/the-difference-between-monosexism-and-biphobia

Esposito, C. (Host). (2018). Gabby Dunn (30) [Audio podcast episode]. In *Queery.* Available at: www.earwolf.com/episode/gaby-dunn

Farrow, H. (2016). *The Bisexual Warriors of the 'Gay' Movement.* [online] Bi.org. Available at: https://bi.org/en/articles/the-bisexual-warriors-of-the-gay-movement

Faye, S. (2018). *Trans Visibility Is Greater than Ever – But That's a Double-Edged Sword.* [online] *The Guardian.* Available at: www.theguardian.com/commentisfree/2018/mar/30/transgender-acceptance-media-international-day-visibility

Fredriksen-Goldsen, K.I., Kim, H.-J., Barkan, S.E., Balsam, K.F. and Mincer, S.L. (2010). Disparities in Health-Related Quality of Life: A Comparison of Lesbians and Bisexual Women. *American Journal of Public Health* 100(11), 2255–2261.

Frieden, T.R., Degutis, L.C., Spivak, H.R., Walters, M.L., Chen, J., and Breiding, M.J. (2012). *The National Intimate Partner and Sexual Violence Survey 2010 Findings on Victimization by Sexual Orientation National Center for Injury Prevention and Control Division of Violence Prevention.* National Center for Injury Prevention and Control. [online] Available at: www.cdc.gov/ violenceprevention/pdf/nisvs_sofindings.pdf

Gates, G.J. (2014). *Food Insecurity and SNAP (Food Stamps) Participation in LGBT Communities.* [online] The Williams Institute. Available at: https:// williamsinstitute.law.ucla.edu/wp-content/uploads/Food-Insecurity-SNAP-Feb-2014.pdf

Gelman, S. (2012). *Annual Reviews Conversations Presents an Interview with Susan Gelman.* [online] *Annual Reviews.* Available at: www.annualreviews.org/ userimages/contenteditor/1345068992315/susangelmantranscript.pdf

GLAAD. (2012). *Where We Are on TV.* [online] Available at: www.glaad.org/files/ whereweareontv12.pdf

GLAAD. (2020). *Where We Are on TV.* [online] Available at: www.glaad.org/sites/ default/files/GLAAD%20WHERE%20WE%20ARE%20ON%20TV%202019%20 2020.pdf

Goldrick-Rab, S., Richardson, J., Schneider, J., Hernandez, A., and Cady, C. (2018). *Still Hungry and Homeless in College.* [online] Available at: https:// hope4college.com/wp-content/uploads/2018/09/Wisconsin-HOPE-Lab-Still-Hungry-and-Homeless.pdf

Gorman, B.K., Denney, J.T., Dowdy, H., and Medeiros, R.A. (2015). A New Piece of the Puzzle: Sexual Orientation, Gender, and Physical Health Status. *Demography,* 52(4), 1357–1382.

Hall, J. (2016). *Tracing the History of the Word 'Queer'.* [online] Dazed. Available at: www.dazeddigital.com/artsandculture/article/32213/1/ tracing-the-history-of-the-word-queer

Harrad, K. (ed.) (2018). *Claiming the B in LGBT: Illuminating the Bisexual Narrative.* Portland, OR: Thorntree Press.

Herek, G.M. (2002). Heterosexuals' Attitudes toward Bisexual Men and Women in the United States. *The Journal of Sex Research* 39(4), 264–274.

Highleyman, L.A. (1995). Identity and Ideas: Strategies for Bisexuals. In Tucker, N., L.A. Highleyman and R. Kaplan (eds), *Bisexual Politics: Theories, Queries, and Vision.* New York: Harrington Park Press.

Holleb, M.L.E. (2019). *The A–Z of Gender and Sexuality.* London: Jessica Kingsley Publishers.

Hogan, H. (2017). *The Lesbophobia Thing.* [online] Available at: https:// heatherannehogan.tumblr.com/post/155299061143/the-lesbophobia-thing

Human Rights Campaign, BiNet USA, Bisexual Resource Center, and Bisexual Organising Project. (n.d.). *Health Disparities Among Bisexual People.* [online] Available at: https://assets2.hrc.org/files/assets/resources/HRC-BiHealth Brief.pdf?_ga=2.261479117.1592207628.1595327725-1032370425.1595327725

Hutchins, L. (2019). Making Bisexuals Visible. In K. Crawford-Lackey and M.E. Springate (eds), *Identities and Place: Changing Labels and Intersectional Communities of LGBTQ and Two-Spirit People in the United States.* New York: Berghahn Books.

Iantffi, A., Barker, M.-J., Van Anders, S., and Scheele, J. (2020). *Mapping Your Sexuality: From Sexual Orientation to Sexual Configuration Theory.* [online] Available at: www.rewriting-the-rules.com/wp-content/uploads/2018/08/MappingYourSexuality.pdf

Jeffries, W.L. (2014). Beyond the Bisexual Bridge. *American Journal of Preventive Medicine,* 47(3), 320–329.

Johnson, N. and Grove, M. (2017). Why Us? Toward an Understanding of Bisexual Women's Vulnerability for and Negative Consequences of Sexual Violence. [online] *Journal of Bisexuality.* Available at: www.researchgate. net/publication/319499700_Why_Us_Toward_an_Understanding_of_Bisexual_Women's_Vulnerability_for_and_Negative_Consequences_of_Sexual_Violence

Jordan, J. (1998). *Affirmative Acts: Political Essays.* New York: Anchor Books.

Joyner, M. (2017). *Monosexism Is Real, We Just Don't Understand It.* [online] Mile Bi Mile. Available at: https://earningmileage.wordpress.com/2017/06/02/monosexism-is-real-we-just-dont-understand-it

Ka'ahumanu, L. (1993). *1993 March on Washington.* [online] Available at: www. lanikaahumanu.com/mow.shtml

Ka'ahumanu, L. and White, M. (2002). *An Introduction to the San Francisco Bay Area Bi+ Community History.* [online] Bay Area Bi+ and Pan Network. Available at: https://www.babpn.org/about.html

Kan, L.M. and Maulbeck, B.F. (2013). *2013 Tracking Report: Lesbian, Gay, Bisexual, Transgender and Queer Grantmaking by U.S. Foundations.* [online] Funders for LGBT Issues. Available at: https://lgbtfunders.org/wp-content/uploads/2018/04/2013_Tracking_Report.pdf.

Klein, F. ([1978] 2014). *The Bisexual Option.* New York: Routledge.

Kumar, A. (2017). *'I Was the First Bisexual Person Granted Asylum in the U.S.,' A First-Person Account for #BiWeek.* [online] GLAAD. Available at: www.glaad.org/blog/i-was-first-bisexual-person-granted-asylum-us-first-person-account-biweek

Lano, K. (1995). Bisexual History: Fighting Invisibility. In S. Rose and C. Stevens (eds), *Bisexual Horizons: Politics, Histories and Lives.* London: Lawrence and Wishart.

Ley, D.J. (2019). Why Are Mental Health Issues Greater Among Bisexual People? [online] *Psychology Today*. Available at: www.psychologytoday.com/gb/blog/women-who-stray/201904/why-are-mental-health-issues-greater-among-bisexual-people

LGBT Foundation. (2020). *The Impact of the Covid-19 Pandemic on LGBT Communities in the UK May 2020 – 3rd Edition*. [online] Available at: https://lgbt.foundation/coronavirus/why-lgbt-people-are-disproportionately-impacted-by-coronavirus

Luna, J. (2018). *I'm Bisexual, I'm Femme, And You Can't Tell Me Otherwise*. [online] *GO Magazine*. Available at: http://gomag.com/article/im-bisexual-im-femme-and-you-cant-tell-me-otherwise

Marks, K., McCarthy, S., Matthewson, T., Mullan, L. and Jovic, M. (2018). *Where Are All the Women?* pwc.com.au.

Marusic, K. (2016). *Why Do So Many Bisexuals End Up In 'Straight' Relationships?* [online] *Slate Magazine*. Available at: https://slate.com/human-interest/2016/05/over-80-percent-of-bisexuals-end-up-in-straight-relationships-why.html

Melani, C. (2019). *Re-imagining Role Models in the Workplace for Bi Women*. [online] SBS. Available at: www.sbs.com.au/topics/sexuality/agenda/article/2018/09/10/re-imagining-role-models-workplace-bi-women

Melville, S., Stonborough, E., and Gooch, B. (2020). *Bi Report LGBT in Britain*. [online] Stonewall. Available at: www.stonewall.org.uk/system/files/lgbt_in_britain_bi.pdf

Mind. (2017). *Stand Bi Me*. [online] Available at: www.mind.org.uk/media-a/3238/stand-bi-me.pdf

Mirza, S.A. (2018). *Disaggregating the Data for Bisexual People*. [online] Center for American Progress. Available at: www.americanprogress.org/issues/lgbtq-rights/reports/2018/09/24/458472/disaggregating-data-bisexual-people

Moon, D. (2016). *How Queerness Erased Bisexuality*. [online] *Medium*. Available at: https://medium.com/@dawnemoon/how-queerness-erased-bisexuality-efc13e1200f4

Morgan, M. (2017, 30 June). If you hear "Bisexual Visibility Day is September 23rd" & don't angrily complain sept- means seven then maybe shut up about bi- means two. [Tweet] Available at: https://twitter.com/MischiefMental/status/880831756613672960

Movement Advancement Project (MAP). (2016). *Invisible Majority: The Disparities Facing Bisexual People and How to Remedy Them*. [online] Movement Advancement Project. Available at: www.lgbtmap.org/file/invisible-majority.pdf

Nelson, L. (2005). *Brenda Howard 1946–2005.* [online] New York Area Bisexual Network. Available at: www.nyabn.org/brenda/others.html

Newsweek Staff (1995). *Bisexuality.* [online] *Newsweek.* Available at: www.newsweek.com/bisexuality-184830

Nordheimer, J. (1987, 3 April). *Aids Specter for Women: The Bisexual Man.* [online] *The New York Times.* 3 April. Available at: www.nytimes.com/1987/04/03/us/aids-specter-for-women-the-bisexual-man.html

Ochs, R. (2014a). *Bisexuality, Feminism, Men and Me.* [online] Robyn Ochs. Available at: https://robynochs.com/bisexuality-feminism-men-and-me

Ochs, R. (2014b). *Selected Quotes by Robyn Ochs.* [online] Robyn Ochs. Available at: https://robynochs.com/quotes

Office for National Statistics. (2018). *Women Most at Risk of Experiencing Partner Abuse in England and Wales.* [online] Available at: www.ons.gov.uk/peoplepopulationandcommunity/crimeandjustice/articles/women mostatriskofexperiencingpartnerabuseinenglandandwales/yearsending march2015to2017#characteristics-of-women-who-are-most-at-risk-of-experiencing-partner-abuse

Payton, N. (2015). *Bisexuals More Likely to Live in Poverty or Have Poor Health.* [online] PinkNews. Available at: www.pinknews.co.uk/2015/07/02/bisexuals-more-likely-to-live-in-poverty-or-have-poor-health

Rankin, S., Morton, J. and Bell, M. (2015). *Complicated? Bisexual People's Experiences of and Ideas for Improving Services.* [online] Available at: www.equality-network.org/wp-content/uploads/2015/04/Complicated-Bisexual-Report.pdf

Rehaag, S. (2009). Bisexuals Need Not Apply: A Comparative Appraisal of Refugee Law and Policy in Canada, the United States, and Australia. [online] *The International Journal of Human Rights.* www.tandfonline.com/doi/abs/10.1080/13642980902758226

Rich, A. (1982). *Compulsory Heterosexuality and Lesbian Existence.* Denver, CO: Antelope Publications.

Robinson, J.P. and Espelage, D.L. (2011). Inequities in Educational and Psychological Outcomes Between LGBTQ and Straight Students in Middle and High School. *Educational Researcher* 40, 7 315–330.

Robinson Rhodes, M. (2020). Bisexuality, Multiple-Gender-Attraction, and Gay Liberation Politics in the 1970s. [online] *Twentieth Century British History.* Available at: https://academic.oup.com/tcbh/advance-article/doi/10.1093/tcbh/hwaa018/5855845?fbclid=IwAR2X--rDIWbcIHbZoU Toe1E_y99ESf_lxnEsqV8cilWMw8ggqYWDu8VtSnU#204562891

Rust, P.C. (1995). *Bisexuality and the Challenge to Lesbian Politics: Sex, Loyalty, and Revolution*. New York: New York University Press.

San Francisco Human Rights Commission (n.d.) *Bisexual Invisibility: Impacts and Recommendations*. [online] Available at: https://sf-hrc.org/sites/default/files/Documents/HRC_Publications/Articles/Bisexual_Invisiblity_Impacts_and_Recommendations_March_2011.pdf

Scarcella, A. (2013, 15 September). What Lesbians Think About Bisexuals. [Video] YouTube. Available at: www.youtube.com/watch?v=xUozcqlhX3w

Schuler, M.S. and Collins, R.L. (2020). Sexual Minority Substance Use Disparities: Bisexual Women at Elevated Risk Relative to Other Sexual Minority Groups. *Drug and Alcohol Dependence*, 206, 107755.

ScienceDaily. (2013). *It May Not 'Get Better' for Bisexual Teens*. [online] *ScienceDaily*. Available at: www.sciencedaily.com/releases/2013/10/131001151046.htm

Seely, E. (n.d.) *Bi Is Enough: Parting with Bisexuality*. [online] *Culture Consent Magazine*. Available at: www.culturalconsent.com/home/bi-is-enough

Serano, J. (2018). *Bisexuality Does Not Reinforce the Gender Binary*. [online] *Scavenger*. Accessed on 01/11/2019 at: www.thescavenger.net/sex-gender-sexual-diversity/glb-diversity/467-bisexuality-does-not-reinforce-the-gender-binary-39675.html

Shearing, L. (2017). *What It's Like to Be Out But Not Out-Out as a Bisexual*. [online] *Medium*. Available at: https://medium.com/@lois.shearing/what-its-like-to-be-out-but-not-out-out-as-a-bisexual-a05a98db935f

Shearing, L. (2018a). *Dear Lesbians, No, I'm Not Gay*. [online] Bi.org. Available at: https://bi.org/en/articles/dear-lesbians-no-im-not-gay

Shearing, L. (2018b). *Bisexual Women Are More Likely to Face Abuse – And No One Is Asking Why*. [online] *The Independent*. Available at: www.independent.co.uk/voices/bisexual-lgbt-pride-sexual-assault-violence-invisible-minority-survivors-a8435226.html

Shearing, L. (2018c). *Seeing Through the Bi Erasure that Swirls Around Cynthia Nixon*. [online] *Medium*. Available at: https://medium.com/@lois.shearing/seeing-through-the-bi-erasure-that-swirls-around-cynthia-nixon-9b438f0eec35

Shearing, L. (2019). *Bisexual Poverty Is Overlooked by the LGBT+ Community*. [online] *Medium*. Available at: https://medium.com/@lois.shearing/bisexual-poverty-is-overlooked-by-the-lgbt-community-9258b04b2334

Sprayregen, M. (2020). *As the Economy Reopens, LGBTQ People Disproportionately Face Employment Challenges, HRC Study Finds*. [online] *Forbes*. Available at: www.forbes.com/sites/mollysprayregen/2020/09/04/as-economies-reopen-lgbtq-people-disproportionately-face-employment-challenges-hrc-study-finds/#4fc0ee937abd

Stonewall. (2018). *Celebrating Bi Inclusion in Secondary Schools*. (2018). [online] Available at: www.stonewall.org.uk/system/files/bi_inclusion_guide.pdf

The Albert Kennedy Trust (n.d.). *LGBT Youth Homelessness: A UK National Scoping of Cause, Prevalence, Response, and Outcome.* [online] Available at: www.theproudtrust.org/resources/research-and-guidance-by-other-organisations/lgbt-youth-homelessness-a-uk-national-scoping-of-cause-prevalence-response-and-outcome

Tracy, M. (2019). *Trans Flag Creator Looks Ahead to WorldPride.* [online] Gay City News. Available at: www.gaycitynews.com/trans-flag-creator-looks-ahead-to-worldpride

Tweedy, A. and Yescavage, K. (2013). Employment Discrimination Against Bisexuals and Others with Fluid Identities. [online] *SSRN Electronic Journal.* Available at: www.researchgate.net/publication/272304059_Employment_Discrimination_against_Bisexuals_and_Others_with_Fluid_Identities

Tweedy, A. and Yescavage, K. (2015). Employment Discrimination Against Bisexuals: An Empirical Study. [online] *William & Mary Journal of Women and the Law.* Available at: http://anntweedy.com/wp-content/uploads/2016/07/Employment-Discrim-opt.pdf

Uhrig, S.C.N. (2014). *An Examination of Poverty and Sexual Orientation in the UK.* [online] Institute for Social and Economic Research University of Essex. Available at: www.iser.essex.ac.uk/research/publications/working-papers/iser/2014-02.pdf

United Nations General Assembly (2018). *Report of the Independent Expert on Protection Against Violence and Discrimination Based on Sexual Orientation and Gender Identity.* [online] United Nations Human Rights Council. Available at: www.un.org/en/ga/search/view_doc.asp?symbol=A/HRC/38/43n

Voss, G., Browne, K., and Gupta, C. (2014). Embracing the 'And': Between Queer and Bi Theory at Brighton BiFest. *Journal of Homosexuality.* Available at: www.academia.edu/2548749/Embracing_the_And_Between_Queer_and_Bi_Theory_at_Brighton_BiFest

Voynovskaya, N. (2020). *How an Unlikely Publicity Stunt at the 1984 DNC Paved the Way for Bi Visibility.* [online] KQED. Available at: www.kqed.org/arts/13882546/how-an-unlikely-publicity-stunt-at-the-1984-dnc-paved-the-way-for-bi-visibility

Vrangalova, Z. (n.d.). *A New Study Explains Why Many Lesbians Are Biased Against Bisexual Women.* [online] *them.* Available at: www.them.us/story/study-explains-lesbian-bias-against-bisexual-women

Walters, M.L., Chen, J., and Breiding, M.J. (2013). *The National Intimate Partner and Sexual Violence Survey 2010 Findings on Victimization by Sexual Orientation.* [online] National Center for Injury Prevention and Control. Available at: www.cdc.gov/violenceprevention/pdf/nisvs_sofindings.pdf

Weinberg, M.S., Pryor, D.W., and Williams, C.J. (1994). *Dual Attraction: Understanding Bisexuality.* New York: Oxford University Press.

Williams, H.S. (2018). Foreword. In K. Harrad (ed.), *Claiming the B in LGBT: Illuminating the Bisexual Narrative.* Portland, OR: Thorntree Press.

Yoshino, K. (2000). The Epistemic Contract of Bisexual Erasure. *Stanford Law Review,* 52(2), 353.

Zane, Z. (2016). *The Silver Lining of Dating When Bi.* [online] Bi.org. Available at: https://bi.org/en/articles/the-silver-lining-of-dating-when-bi

Zane, Z. (2017). *You Are Not Responsible for the 'Bi Brand'.* [online] Bi.org. Available at: https://bi.org/en/articles/you-are-not-responsible-for-the-bi-brand

Zane, Z. (2018). *Good Bi Love: You Can Still Have Preferences.* [online] Bi.org. Available at: https://bi.org/en/articles/good-bi-love-you-can-still-have-preferences

Resources That Informed the Text

akt. (n.d.). *What We Do.* [online] Available at: www.akt.org.uk/what-we-do

Alptraum, L. (n.d.). *How Do Bi Parents Come Out to Their Kids?* [online] SELF. Available at: www.self.com/story/bi-parent-coming-out

Anderlini-D'Onofrio, S. (2003). *Women and Bisexuality: A Global Perspective.* New York: Haworth Press.

Antjoule, N. (2016). *Tacking Biphobia: A Guide for Safety Services.* [online] Galop. Available at: www.lgbthatecrime.org.uk/assets/downloads/10%20Tacking%20Biphobia%20-%20A%20Guide%20for%20Safety%20Services.pdf

Beemyn, B.G. (2004). *Bisexual Movements.* [online] Available at: www.glbtqarchive.com/ssh/bisex_movements_S.pdf

Bialogue. (n.d.). *Bialogue: Bisexual + Queer Politics.* [online] Available at: https://bialogue-group.tumblr.com/post/86421457765/bisexual-community-celebrating-10-years-of

Bisexual/Non-Monosexual & Queer Community. (n.d.). *Bisexual/Non-Monosexual & Queer Community.* [online] Available at: https://bisexual-community.tumblr.com/post/122633707813/bisexual-pride-marriage-equality-perfect

Bowie, A. (2002). *Bisexuality (Pocket Essential series).* Harpenden, UK: Pocket Essentials.

Cheltenham, F. (2015). *The Bisexual History of HIV/AIDS, in Photos.* [online] LGBT HealthLink. Available at: https://blog.lgbthealthlink.org/2015/01/29/the-bisexual-history-of-hivaids-in-photos

Orna, I. (1995). If Half of You Dodges a Bullet, All of You Ends up Dead. In L.A. Highleyman and R. Kaplan (eds), *Bisexual Politcs: Theories, Queries, and Vision.* New York: Harrington Park Press.

Crawford-Lackey, K. and Springate, M.E. (2019). *Identities and Place: Changing Labels and Intersectional Communities of LGBTQ and Two-Spirit People in the United States*. New York: Berghahn.

Cruz, E. (2014). *Study: Biphobia Puts Bisexual Men at Risk for STIs*. [online] the Advocate. Available at: www.advocate.com/bisexuality/2014/06/26/study-biphobia-puts-bisexual-men-risk-stis

Cruz, E. (2015). *Report: Bisexuals Face Biphobia at Doctor's Office, LGBT Groups*. [online] *The Advocate*. Available at: www.advocate.com/bisexuality/2015/05/27/report-bisexuals-face-biphobia-doctors-office-lgbt-groups

Cruz, E. (2017). *'Double Discrimination' and Loneliness Contribute to Bisexual Health Disparities, Study Says*. [online] NBC News. Available at: www.nbcnews.com/feature/nbc-out/double-discrimination-loneliness-contribute-bisexual-health-disparities-study-says-n798071

Cruz, E. (2019). *Bisexual Pioneer Brenda Howard Is the Mother of Pride*. [online] *The Advocate*. Available at: www.advocate.com/bisexuality/2014/06/17/remembering-brenda-ode-%E2%80%98mother-pride%E2%80%99

Cunningham, N. (2011). *Lesbian, Gay, Bisexual, Transgender and Queer Grantmaking by U.S. Foundations*. [online] Funders for LGBT Issues. Available at: https://lgbtfunders.org/wp-content/uploads/2018/04/2011LGBTQGrantmaking Report.pdf

Dias, A. (2018). *Young Bisexual Men Are the Least Likely to Have Come Out, triple j Survey Finds*. [online] triple j. Available at: www.abc.net.au/triplej/programs/hack/triple-j-whats-up-in-your-world-survey-on-coming-out-bisexual/10058348

Dingle, C. (2017). *Bisexuality and Preference*. [online] Curve Magazine. Available at: www.curvemag.com/sexuality/bisexual/preference-and-bisexuality

Eisner, S. (2011). *Words, Binary and Biphobia, Or: Why 'Bi' Is Binary but 'FTM' Is Not*. [online] Bi Radical. Available at: https://radicalbi.wordpress.com/2011/02/22/words-binary-and-biphobia-or-why-bi-is-binary-but-ftm-is-not

Eliason, M.J. (2001). *Bi-Negativity*. [online] *Journal of Bisexuality*. Available at: www.researchgate.net/publication/233112650_Bi-Negativity

Erickson-Schroth, L. and Mitchell, J. (2009). Queering Queer Theory, or Why Bisexuality Matters. *Journal of Bisexuality*, 9(3–4), 297–315.

Gattuso, R. (2020). *Why Are Bisexual Women at a Higher Risk of Substance Abuse?* [online] *Talkspace*. Available at: www.talkspace.com/blog/lgbtq-addiction-bisexual-women

Goodman, E. (2019). *Meet 'The Mother of Pride', the Pioneering Bisexual Activist Brenda Howard*. [online] them. Available at: www.them.us/story/brenda-howard

Greenesmith, H. (2018a). *High Risk, Few Resources: Bisexual Kids Lack Help When They Need It Most.* [online] *Rewire News.* Available at: https://rewire.news/article/2018/04/04/high-risk-resources-bisexual-kids-lack-help-need

Greenesmith, H. (2018b). *The Truth About Bisexual College Students and Hunger.* [online] *HuffPost.* Available at: www.huffpost.com/entry/opinion-greenesmith-bisexual-youth-homelessness-hunger_n_5ad0d64ee4b016a07e9c08d8

Greenesmith, H. (2018c). *We Know Biphobia Is Harmful. But Do We Know What's Behind It?* [online] *Rewire News.* Available at: https://rewire.news/article/2018/04/25/know-biphobia-harmful-know-whats-behind

Hemmings, C. (2002). *Bisexual Spaces: A Geography of Sexuality and Gender.* New York: Routledge.

Hoke, C. (2017). *Michael Page: Bisexual Pride Flag (1998).* [online] Queer Art History. Available at: www.queerarthistory.com/uncategorized/michael-page-bisexual-pride-flag-1998

Holden, K. (n.d.). *Letter to the Thistle: Bisexuality and Feminism.* [online] *The Thistle.* Available at: http://web.mit.edu/thistle/www/v9/9.06/4bisexuality.html

Hsieh, N. and Liu, H. (2019). *Marriage Could be Good for Your Health – Unless You're Bisexual.* [online] *The Conversation.* Available at: https://theconversation.com/marriage-could-be-good-for-your-health-unless-youre-bisexual-121865

Human Rights Campaign. (2015). *Bisexual FAQ.* [online] Available at: www.hrc.org/resources/bisexual-faq

Jagannathan, M. (2019). *1 in 5 LGBTQ Americans Lives in Poverty – And Some Groups Are Particularly Worse Off.* [online] *MarketWatch.* Available at: www.marketwatch.com/story/1-in-5-lgbtq-americans-lives-in-poverty-and-some-groups-are-particularly-worse-off-2019-10-22

Kan, L.M. and Wallace, A. (2018). *2018 Tracking Report: LGBTQ Grantmaking by U.S Foundations.* [online] Funders for LGBT Issues. Available at: https://lgbtfunders.org/wp-content/uploads/2018/02/2020.04.02_FINAL_2018TrackingReport_08.pdf

Lafuente, C. (2019). *The Truth About the Trans Flag.* [online] TheList.com. Available at: www.thelist.com/158406/the-truth-about-the-trans-flag

Maliepaard, E. (2015). Bisexual Spaces: Exploring Geographies of Bisexualities. [online] *ACME: An International Journal for Critical Geographies.* Available at: https://acme-journal.org/index.php/acme/article/view/1148

Marcus, N. (2015). Bridging Bisexual Erasure in LGBT-Rights Discourse and Litigation. *Michigan Journal of Gender & Law.* [online]. Available at: https://repository.law.umich.edu/cgi/viewcontent.cgi?article=1052&context=mjgl

Maulbeck, B.F. and Kan, L.M. (2012). *2012 Tracking Report: LGBTQ Grantmaking By U.S. Foundations*. [online] Funders for LGBT Issues. Available at: https://lgbtfunders.org/research-item/lgbtq-grantmaking-2012

Morgan, J. (2018). *Ignorant Judges Are Sending Bisexual Asylum Seekers to Their Deaths*. [online] *Gay Star News*. Available at: www.gaystarnews.com/article/ignorant-judges-officials-sending-bisexual-asylum-seekers-deaths

Napikoski, L. (2019). *Feminists Question Compulsory Heterosexuality*. [online] *ThoughtCo*. Available at: www.thoughtco.com/compulsory-heterosexuality-overview-3528951

Oded, Y. (2019). *Good to Know: Robyn Ochs and Her Fight for the Bi+ Community*. [online] *Screen Shot*. Available at: https://screenshot-media.com/politics/lgbtqi-rights/bi-visibility-robyn-ochs

Orna, I. (1995). If Half of You Dodges a Bullet, All of You Ends up Dead. In: L.A. Highleyman and R. Kaplan, eds., *Bisexual Politcs Theories, Queries, & vision*. New York: Harrington Park Press.

Parker, K. (2015). *Among LGBT Americans, Bisexuals Stand Out When It Comes to Identity, Acceptance*. [online] Pew Research Center. Available at: www.pewresearch.org/fact-tank/2015/02/20/among-lgbt-americans-bisexuals-stand-out-when-it-comes-to-identity-acceptance

Pell, S. (2002). Inescapable Essentialism: Bisexually-Identified Women's Strategies in the Late 80s and Early 90s. [online] *Thirdspace*. Available at: https://journals.sfu.ca/thirdspace/index.php/journal/article/view/pell/64

Picker, C. (2019). *Bi-Visibility: How the Media Plays a Part in Bi-Erasure*. [online] *The Bubble*. Available at: www.thebubble.org.uk/lifestyle/sex/bi-visibility-how-the-media-plays-a-part-in-bi-erasure

Rainbow History Project Digital Collections (n.d.). *ABilly S. Jones-Hennin*. [online] Available at: https://archives.rainbowhistory.org/exhibits/show/pioneers/2007awardees/jones-hennin

Rawlings-Fein, M. (2017). *Who Is Counted? Why When We Rise Matters*. [online] Bay Area Bi+ and Pan Network. Available at: www.bayareabisexualnetwork.org/blog/who-is-counted-why-when-we-rise-matters

Rosenblum, M. (2017). *The U.S. Bisexual+ Movement: A #BiWeek history lesson*. [online] GLAAD. Available at: www.glaad.org/blog/us-bisexual-movement-biweek-history-lesson

Sharpe, B. (2020). *Why Bisexual and Pansexual Parents Struggle to Find Community*. [online] *HuffPost Canada*. Available at: www.huffingtonpost.ca/entry/bisexual-parents-prejudices-seeking-community_ca_5f523d7ec5b6946f3ebobae6

Shearing, L. (2016). The bisexual erasure/over-sexualisation feedback loop. [online] *The Queerness*. Available at: https://thequeerness.com/2016/12/21/the-bisexual-erasure-over-sexualisation-feedback-loop

Still Bisexual (n.d.). *Who We Are*. [online] Available at: https://stillbisexual.com/who-we-are

Townsend, M. (2019). *GLAAD's 'Where We Are on TV' Report Shows TV Is Telling More LGBTQ Stories Than Ever*. [online] GLAAD. Available at: www.glaad.org/blog/glaads-where-we-are-tv-report-shows-tv-telling-more-lgbtq-stories-ever

Tucker, N. (1996). *Bisexual Politics: Theories, Queries, and Visions*. London: Routledge.

Wallace, A., Nepon, E. and Postic, J. (2020). *2017-2018 Global Resources Report*. [online] Funders for LGBT Issues. Available at: https://lgbtfunders.org/research-item/2017-2018-global-resources-report

Wallace, A., Maulbeck, B.F. and Kan, L.M. (2018). *2016 Tracking Report*. [online] Funders for LGBT Issues. Available at: https://lgbtfunders.org/research-item/2016-tracking-report

Welzer-Lang, D. (2008). Speaking Out Loud About Bisexuality: Biphobia in the Gay and Lesbian Community. [online] *Journal of Bisexuality*. Available at: www.researchgate.net/publication/232835557_Speaking_Out_Loud_About_Bisexuality_Biphobia_in_the_Gay_and_Lesbian_Community

Whitbeck, L., Lazoritz, M.W., Crawford, D. and Hautala, D. (2016). *Administration for Children and Families Family and Youth Services Bureau Street Outreach Program*. [online] Available at: www.acf.hhs.gov/sites/default/files/fysb/data_collection_study_final_report_street_outreach_program.pdf

Winfred, T. (2017). *Examining the Issue of Bisexual Visibility and Erasure in LGBTQ Media*. [online] The Good Men Project. Available at: https://goodmenproject.com/featured-content/examining-issue-bisexual-visibility-erasure-lgbtq-media-lbkr

Zane, Z. (2017). In the LGBT Community, Bisexual People Have More Health Risks. Here's What Could Help. [online] *Washington Post*. Available at: www.washingtonpost.com/news/soloish/wp/2017/09/25/in-the-lgbt-community-bisexual-people-have-more-health-risks-heres-what-could-help

Index